WINDOWS 98

in easy steps

HARSHAD KOTECHA

COMPUTER
STEP

In easy steps is an imprint of Computer Step
Southfield Road . Southam
Warwickshire CV47 OFB . England

http://www.ineasysteps.com

Notice of Liability

Every effort has been made to ensure that this book contains accurate
and current information. However, Computer Step and the author shall
not be liable for any loss or damage suffered by readers as a result of
any information contained herein.

Trademarks

Microsoft® and Windows® are registered trademarks of Microsoft
Corporation. All other trademarks are acknowledged as belonging to
their respective companies.

Printed and bound in the United Kingdom

ISBN 1-874029-70-9

Table Of Contents

First Steps

This chapter shows you how to start and shut down Windows 98. You'll learn how to use the Start button, and how to switch between Classic/Web views. Finally, you'll use the extensive on-line help system (including troubleshooters and on-line technical support).

Covers

Chapter One

Introduction

Microsoft Windows 98 is an upgrade of the following operating systems used on personal computers:

Windows 98 is Year 2000 ready.

- MS-DOS
- Microsoft Windows for Workgroups 3.11
- Microsoft Windows 3.1 and 95

Windows 98 builds on features already incorporated into Windows 95 and adds to them. Some of the main innovations include:

Windows 98 also has a special utility – FAT 32 – which increases the amount of available hard disk space (without data compression) and makes programs run more quickly (see chapter 12).

- Improved interface (you can have Windows 98 look and act like the Internet, so that – for instance – programs can be launched with a single mouse click) – see pages 11, 13, 14

- Internet access is even easier for new users

- Support for multiple monitors

- Programs launch more rapidly

- Adding peripherals is easier with USB (Universal Serial Bus) support

- Better multimedia and game support

Another new feature is support for DVD optical storage.
DVD (Digital Versatile Disc) is the natural enhancement of the CD-ROM – it's capable of storing a full-length feature movie.

- The use of wizards is much enhanced. For example, you can keep your PC up-to-date with the latest driver and operating system updates by having the Windows Update wizard download new files for you. And the Maintenance wizard ensures your system is always running at peak performance.

The basic foundation underlying any version of Windows is its 'windowing' capability. A window (spelt with a lower-case w) is a rectangular area used to display information or to run a program. Several windows can be opened at the same time to work with multiple applications, so you should be able to dramatically increase your productivity when using your computer.

Using a Mouse

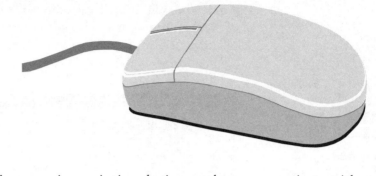

The great advantage of using the Internet in Windows 98 is that you can access it in a wide variety of ways. These include:

- *Internet Explorer directly*
- *Windows Explorer*
- *Active Desktop, Windows logo in any folder, Address/Links toolbar*
- *Internet shortcuts*
- *Favorites*
- *Channels*

A mouse is a pointing device used to communicate with your computer. It is recommended that you use a Microsoft, or Microsoft-compatible, mouse with *Windows 98*.

To use it, first place it on a flat surface or use a mouse mat. You will notice an arrow-headed pointer ( ) moving on your screen as you move the mouse.

To make a selection, move the mouse pointer on top of an item and then press and release (or click) the left mouse button (classic view), or simply rest the mouse pointer over an item for a few seconds (web view). Sometimes you can click twice in rapid succession (double-click) to select an item in classic view or single-click in web view.

A mouse will usually have at least one more button on the right (called the right mouse button). This provides further facilities – for example, a right-click of the mouse button when it is over an appropriate object will display a shortcut menu of related options for further selection.

Wherever (in later chapters) tips explain that operations require a live Internet connection, this means one of the following:

- *a modem attached to your PC*
- *an ISDN line*
- *a leased line*

A mouse can also be used to move items on the screen. This is achieved by first moving the mouse pointer over an item. Then, press and hold down the left mouse button and move the mouse to position the item. Finally, once you see the item in the new location, release the mouse button. This technique is called 'dragging'.

In this guide we will use the terms: Click, Double-click, Right-click and Drag to refer to mouse operations described above.

Starting Windows 98

After you switch on your computer you may be asked to log on to Windows (or to the network if your computer is linked to others). Simply type in your password and click OK.

Change your password by selecting Start menu, Settings, Control Panel,

Passwords.

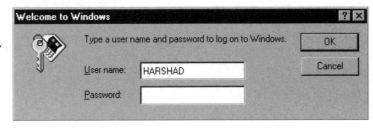

Then the Welcome window is displayed on the desktop:

Click this button to close the window

Click here if you don't want to see this window each time you start

Windows.

The Welcome window is useful, especially for a beginner. Click on Discover Windows 98 (and follow the instructions on screen) to get a basic 'feel' of the features available in Windows 98.

The other options – Register Now, Connect to the Internet and Maintain Your Computer – launch self-explanatory wizards. (See pages 22-23 for more information on wizards in general).

The Desktop

If you haven't upgraded from a previous installation, your Windows 98 desktop should only have a few *icons* from which all tasks can be performed easily. As a result, most of the desktop is a tidy blank area.

Channel Bar (see chapter 7)

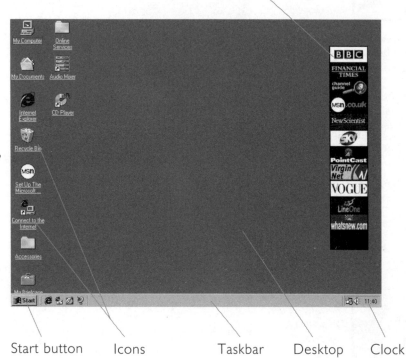

Start button   Icons   Taskbar   Desktop   Clock

Single-click on any icon to launch a major facility available in Windows 98 – you can create your own shortcut icons for frequent programs that you'll be using.

Single-click the Start button to access and run all your programs, change settings and use the Help system.

The Taskbar at the bottom can be moved to any of the other three edges of the desktop. A Task button is created on here automatically for every program running – click on it to switch between them.

The Start Button

The Start button on the Taskbar is designed with the beginner in mind, and allows you to select and start a program quickly just with a single mouse click. Other common tasks that you need to do using your computer are also available directly from the Start button.

You can also start programs by single-clicking on desktop icons, providing Web style view is in force – see the HOT TIP on page 11, and pages 13-14.

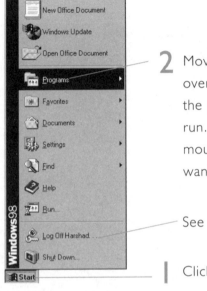

2 Move the mouse arrow over this option to see all the programs you can run. Single click with the mouse on the one you want to start.

See page 24

1 Click on the Start button.

See Chapter 12 for how to use Windows Update.

The Start button options also include:

Windows Update	Updates system files automatically
Favorites	Accesses bookmarked web sites
Documents	Lets you open one of the 15 most recent documents you've been working on. Also accesses My Documents folder
Settings	Lets you change computer settings
Find	A sophisticated search facility
Help	A complete on-line Help system
Run	Used to start a program
Shut Down	A safe way to switch off your computer

Switching Views

You can use the Start button to switch between Web Style and Classic Style views.

Windows 98 provides two views:

* *Web style*

* *Classic style*

When Classic style view is operative, Windows looks and behaves like Windows 95. Web style view, on the other hand, makes your desktop look – and work – like a World Wide Web page.

Additionally, you can combine elements of both views – see page 14.

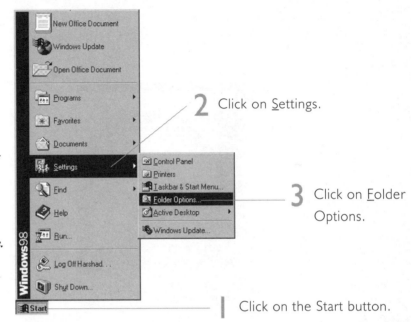

2 Click on Settings.

3 Click on Folder Options.

Click on the Start button.

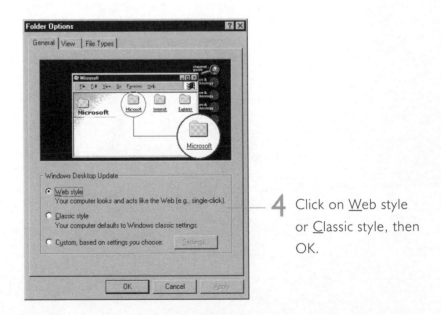

4 Click on Web style or Classic style, then OK.

Customising Views

You can adapt the view chosen in step 4 on page 13. For instance, you can specify whether or not Windows regards folders as Web pages, or only those you've selected.

1 Carry out steps 1–3 on page 13.

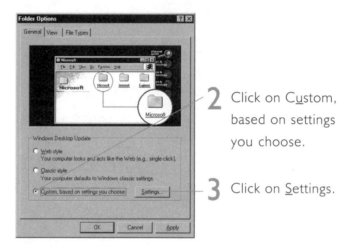

2 Click on Custom, based on settings you choose.

3 Click on Settings.

4 Complete the dialog below. Then click on OK.

5 Click on this button: Close

On-line Help

The Windows 98 Help system has been completely redesigned and improved. Choose <u>H</u>elp from the Start button, or <u>H</u>elp Topics from the <u>H</u>elp menu on some of the windows.

Higher level help is available from the Contents tab, or specific word-based help from Search.

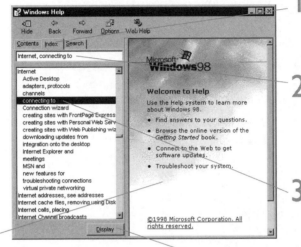

1 Click on the Index tab if not selected.

2 Type key letters of the word you want help on.

3 Click on the appropriate matching phrase.

This is the topic window.

4 Click to display an outline help window for the topic chosen.

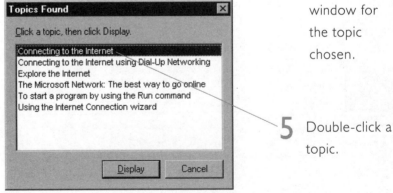

Sometimes, step 5 is not required: the desired topic appears immediately in the topic window.

5 Double-click a topic.

After step 5, the topic you've selected appears in the topic window.

Shortcuts look like this:

Click here

Click on underlined text (apart from Click here) for its definition.

Click on the Back button to return to the previous topic. Click on the Forward button – if available – to jump to a more recent topic.

You can also launch this dialog by double-clicking the Clock on the Taskbar.

Shortcuts

Many Help windows contain Shortcuts (see the HOT TIP on the immediate left). Clicking on a Shortcut will directly display the actual referenced window. For example, if you are getting help on how to change your computer's date, you can change it there and then as you are reading about it.

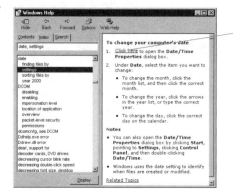

Click on this Shortcut.

2 Change the Date (and/or time) by clicking on the appropriate arrows or the day in the calendar.

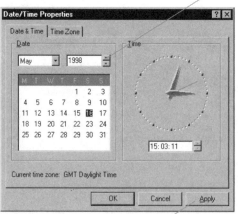

3 Click to confirm the new date/time, or click on OK to achieve the same and close this window.

? button

Many windows will have a ?️ button. Use this to display an explanation of any object on the screen.

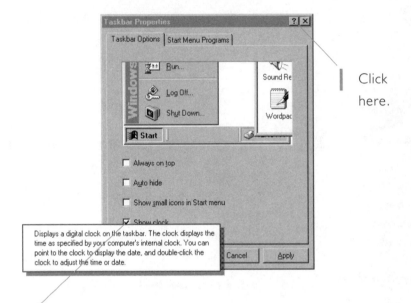

Click here.

2 With your mouse pointer changed to ↖? click on any object in the same window for an explanation of it.

3 Click anywhere to close the explanation box.

Troubleshooters

Windows 98 has an additional HELP feature: troubleshooters. Troubleshooters help you diagnose and fix technical problems.

I Choose Help from the Start button.

2 Click on the Index tab if not selected.

Software and hardware topics covered by troubleshooters include:

- *networking*
- *modems*
- *printing*
- *memory*
- *display*
- *sound*
- *hardware conflicts*

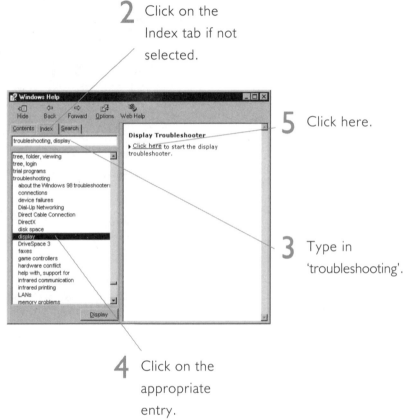

5 Click here.

3 Type in 'troubleshooting'.

4 Click on the appropriate entry.

6 Follow steps 7–9 on page 19.

...cont'd

Consider clicking on this button: 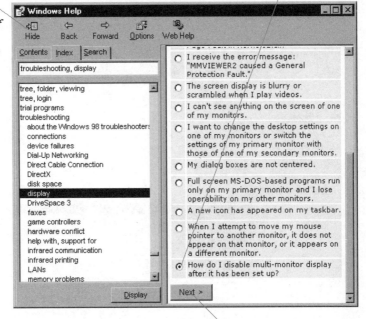 *to hide the Index section of the HELP window (this makes it easier to work with the selected troubleshooter).*

7 Click on a troubleshooting topic.

Ensure you complete the instructions in the topic window accurately.

8 Click on Next.

When you've finished using one or more troubleshooters, press Alt+F4 to close the HELP window.

9 Complete any additional windows which launch, as appropriate.

On-line Technical Support

If you have access to the Internet (e.g. via a service provider such as MSN), you can use Microsoft's on-line Technical Support site to answer technical questions.

1 Ensure your Internet connection is live.

2 Choose Help from the Start button.

See chapter 12 for how to produce diagnostic files, and transmit them to a technical support specialist.

3 Click on the Index tab if not selected.

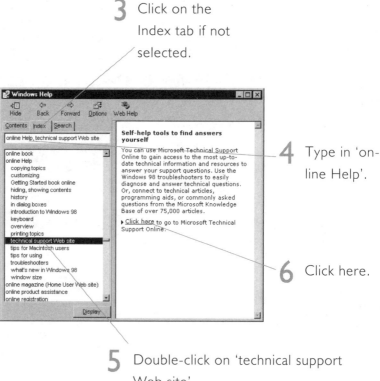

4 Type in 'on-line Help'.

6 Click here.

5 Double-click on 'technical support Web site'.

7 Follow steps 8–10 on page 21.

...cont'd

8 Complete this (and later) registration fields.

Remember to close your Internet connection when you've finished.

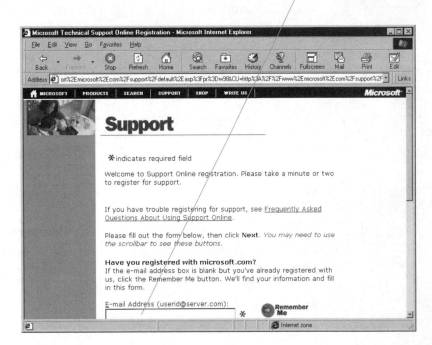

9 Click on the Next button at the base of the above screen.

10 Follow the on-line instructions.

Wizards

Wizards can be used to install other devices, like a modem or fax, or to install a new application. Even the Installation of Windows 98 itself is made easy with the help of Wizards.

If you have been using Microsoft Word or Microsoft Excel, or indeed Windows 95, you will already be familiar with Wizards. These guide you through a series of questions and enable you to complete a complicated task. The best way to illustrate the way Wizards work is with an example. Assume that you wanted to install a printer to work with your computer:

1 Select Printers either from the Settings option available from the Start button, or from the Control Panel window.

If you're currently using Classic style view, double-click (rather than single-click) in step 2.

2 Click on the Add Printer icon to install a new printer.

3 Follow the instructions given in a series of boxes.

Windows 98 has many new wizards e.g. Maintenance wizard (see chapter 12).

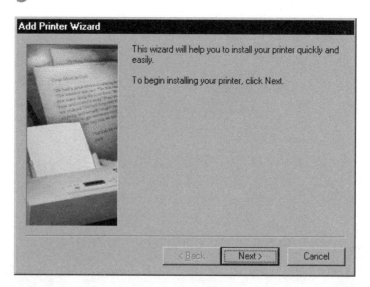

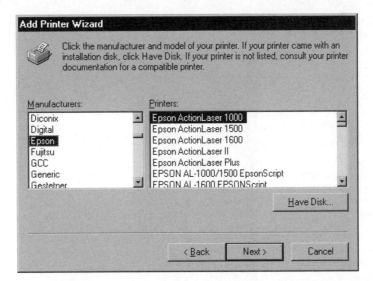

These are further dialogs in the Add Printer Wizard...

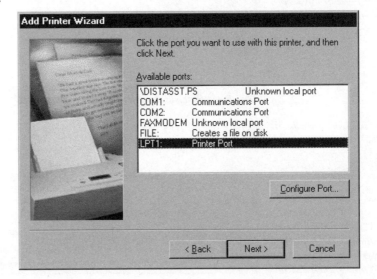

4 Click on the Back button to change options from the previous box, or Cancel to abandon the procedure altogether. Otherwise, continue to complete the dialogs, selecting Next until the last box which replaces this button with Finish. Then click on Finish.

Shutting Down your Computer and Windows 98

If your PC has been set up for multiple users (see chapter 10), you may wish to 'log off' (rather than close down your machine) so another user can use it.
    Click here:
instead of performing step 1. Follow the on-screen instructions.

Click on the Start button, and then on Sh<u>u</u>t Down...

Only switch off when the message, "It's now safe to turn off your computer" is displayed on your screen. (If you have a newer PC with Power management, this message may not appear – instead, your machine should switch off automatically.)

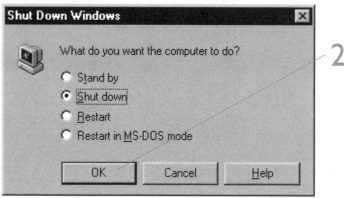

2 Click on OK.

Normally you'll select the <u>S</u>hut down option. A message, "Windows is shutting down", is then displayed. This is when Windows checks if any changes to your documents are saved and prompts you if they're not. It then saves its own settings and closes all the files properly. The S<u>t</u>and by option is optional if your computer uses ACPI (see Power Management in chapter 12).

Basic Controls

Everything you do in Windows 98 will be done using a menu, dialog box or a window. This chapter shows you how you can use these structures.

Covers

Chapter Two

Menus

Many of the windows will have a Menu bar near the top, displaying the menu options relevant to a particular window. Simply click on a menu option to reveal a drop-down list of further options within it. As an example, we will look at the View menu from the My Computer window:

A tick shows that an option is active.

A bullet also shows an option to be active but only one option can be selected from a group. Clicking another option from the group will automatically turn off the previously selected one.

View
Toolbars ▸
✓ Status Bar
Explorer Bar ▸
✓ as Web Page
• Large Icons
Small Icons
List
Details
Arrange Icons ▸
Line Up Icons
Refresh
Folder Options...

by Drive Letter
by Type
by Size
by Free Space
Auto Arrange

A forward arrow indicates that there is another linked menu for selection. Move the mouse arrow onto the option to see it.

The ellipse (i.e. ...) indicates that if this option is selected, an associated window with further selections will be displayed.

Some examples of shortcut keys are:

Ctrl+C — COPY

Ctrl+X — CUT

Ctrl+V — PASTE

See page 52 for more information on these commands.

To deactivate an option with a tick next to it, click on it. Click on it again to activate it.

If an option is dimmed out, it cannot be used at that particular time or is not appropriate.

Some options may have shortcut keys next to them so you can use these instead of clicking on them with your mouse.

Dialog boxes

Although simple settings can be made quickly from menu options, other settings need to be made from windows displayed specifically for this purpose. These are called dialog boxes.

Tabs

Click on the appropriate one to display its settings.

Check boxes

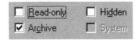

Click on as many as required. A tick indicates that the option is active. If you click on it again it will be turned off. If an option is dimmed out, it cannot be selected.

Radio buttons

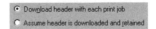

Only one out of a group of radio buttons can be selected. If you click on another radio button, the previously selected one is automatically turned off.

Action buttons

OK will save the settings selected and close the dialog box or window. Cancel will close the window without saving the amended settings – click on it if you've made a mistake. Apply will save the settings selected so far but will not close the window, in case you want to make further changes.

Structure of a window

 Dialog boxes are usually fixed-size windows and therefore don't have scroll bars, minimise, maximise, restore buttons or the control icon. They also don't display resize pointers at the edges.

All windows are similar in their structure. You can have a window containing icons for further selection, or a window that displays a screen from a program.

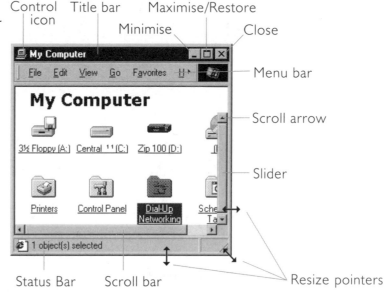

Control icon · Title bar · Maximise/Restore · Minimise · Close · Menu bar · Scroll arrow · Slider · Resize pointers · Status Bar · Scroll bar

 To hide the Status Bar, click on Status Bar from the View menu.

Click on an icon to open a window relating to it.

 If you're currently using the Classic style (rather than Web style) view, double-click (rather than single-click) icons to open the relevant windows. (See pages 13-14 for more information on views.)

From the View menu, click on Toolbars (and then an entry in the sub-menu) to display further buttons under the menu bar.

The Status Bar displays information about items selected from the window.

The scroll bars will only appear when (as here) there are items that cannot fit into the current size of the window.

If you move the mouse pointer over any edge of a window, the pointer changes shape and becomes a double-headed resize pointer – drag it to change the size of a window. (See page 32 – Resizing a window).

Moving a window

As long as a window is not maximised, occupying the whole screen, you can move it. This is especially useful if you have several windows open and need to organise your desktop.

You can have Windows 98 move the whole window as you drag the mouse, instead of just the frame.

Right-click on the desktop and click on Properties from the shortcut menu displayed. This will bring up the Display Properties dialog box – click on the Effects tab. Ensure 'Show window contents while dragging' is selected.

Finally, click on OK.

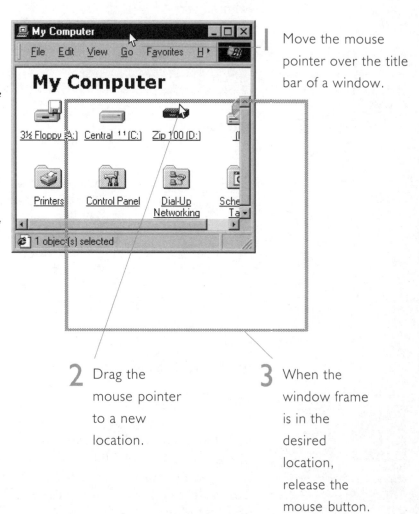

1 Move the mouse pointer over the title bar of a window.

2 Drag the mouse pointer to a new location.

3 When the window frame is in the desired location, release the mouse button.

Maximising, Minimising and Restoring a window

A window can be maximised to fill the whole screen, minimised to a button on the Taskbar, or restored to the original size.

You can also double-click on the Title bar to maximise the window.

Maximised window Minimise button Restore button

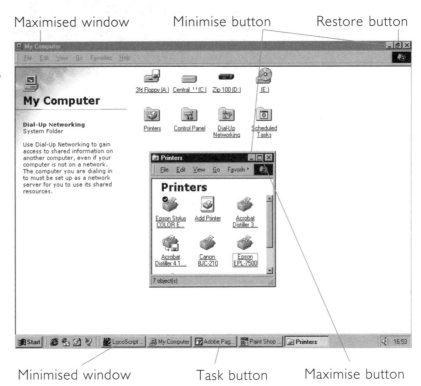

Minimised window Task button Maximise button

Click the Control icon (top left) or right-click the Task button, to display a shortcut menu that also allows you to minimise, maximise and restore the window.

Whether a window is maximised or original size, click on the minimise button (left of the top-right three buttons) to reduce the window to only a Task button on the Taskbar. This will create space on the desktop for you to work on other windows. When you want to restore the reduced window, simply click on it from the Taskbar.

The middle button (out of the three) can either be a maximise button, or – if the window is already maximised – the same button changes to a restore button.

Switching between windows

Switching between windows cannot be easier. The task (window) that is active always has its Title bar highlighted. If you have more than one window displayed on the desktop, click anywhere inside a window that is not active to activate it or switch to it.

active task button   active window

If you have too many windows open, Task buttons will resize themselves automatically.

Press the Alt+Tab keys to toggle and switch between tasks.

Another method of 'task switching' is to use the Taskbar at the bottom. Every window that is open has a button created automatically on the Taskbar. Therefore, it does not matter if the window you want to switch to is overlaid with others and you cannot see it. Just click on the button for it in the Taskbar and the window will appear on top and it will be active.

Resizing a window

As long as a window is not maximised or minimised, it can be resized.

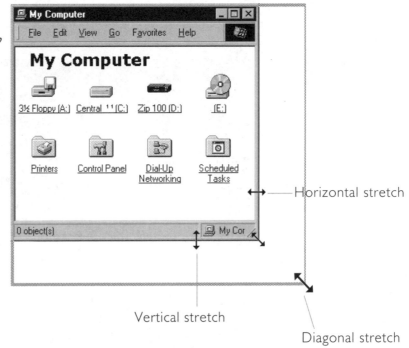

Horizontal stretch

Vertical stretch

Diagonal stretch

1 Place the mouse arrow anywhere on the edge of a window (including corners) – it will change to a double-headed resize pointer.

2 Drag the pointer outwards to increase the size of the window, or inwards to reduce the size.

3 When the outline is in the correct position, release the mouse button – the window will now occupy the area previously shown by the outline.

Arranging windows

If you have several windows open on your desktop and want to automatically rearrange them neatly, rather than resize and move each one individually, use the Cascade or Tile options.

To avoid cluttering your desktop, try not to use the Cascade and Tile options – it is better to use the Minimize All Windows option.

Click on Undo... (where the dots represent the original command) to restore your windows to how they were before you rearranged them.

Right-click on the Taskbar to display a shortcut menu.

2 Click on Cascade Windows (overlaps all the windows so that just the Title bars are visible, except for the front one), Tile Windows Horizontally (resizes each window equally and displays them across the screen in rows), or Tile Windows Vertically (resizes each window equally and displays them across the screen in columns).

Arranging icons

If you have icons displayed (large or small) in a window, you can rearrange the order, either manually or automatically.

Manually

Drag an icon to any space within a window.

Automatically

You can drag an icon out of the window and onto the desktop or another window.

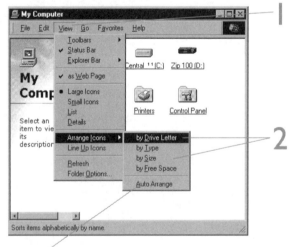

Click on the <u>V</u>iew menu, and move the pointer over Arrange <u>I</u>cons.

2 Click on an option to neatly arrange all the icons in a preferred sequence.

3 Click on <u>A</u>uto Arrange to activate it with a tick, so that if you resize the window, the icons are rearranged automatically.

Scrolling

If a window is not big enough to display all the information within it, then Scroll bars will appear automatically – either vertical, horizontal, or both. Use these to see the contents of a window not immediately in view.

The size of the Slider in relation to the Scroll bar indicates how much of the total contents are in view. The position tells you which portion is in view.

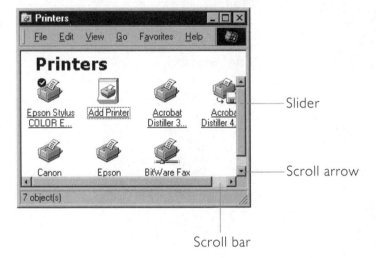

Slider

Scroll arrow

Scroll bar

| Drag the Slider along the Scroll bar towards one of the two Scroll arrows to scroll in that direction.

or

2 Click on the Scroll bar to scroll just a little towards the Scroll arrow nearest to it.

or

3 Click on one of the Scroll arrows to scroll just a little in that direction. Hold down your mouse button to scroll continuously.

Closing a window

When you have finished with a window you will need to close it. There are many ways of doing this – use the method you find the easiest.

 Click on the Close button (top right corner).

If Minimised

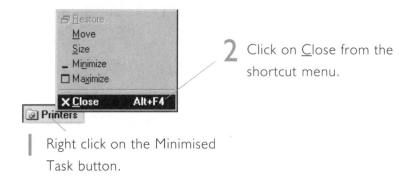

2 Click on Close from the shortcut menu.

Right click on the Minimised Task button.

From the Control icon

Click on the Control icon (top left corner).

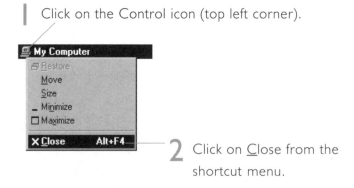

2 Click on Close from the shortcut menu.

From the keyboard

Press Alt+F4 to close the active window.

Working with Programs

Most of the time you'll be using your computer to run a program or an application you have installed. Find out how to start programs and how Windows 98 can help you organise them for fast, easy access.

Covers

Chapter Three

Starting and Closing Programs

The Start button enables you to quickly start any program listed under the Programs option. You can add new programs to this list, or remove entries for programs not used very frequently (shown later in this chapter).

If you are using a program frequently, drag its icon onto the Start button and it will appear at the top of the Start menu for an even quicker start to that program.

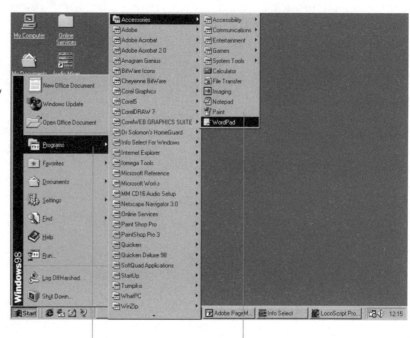

1 Click on Start and move the mouse pointer over the Programs option.

2 Click on a Program name you want to start. A name with a forward-arrow is a program group rather than an actual program. Move the pointer over it to display a cascaded menu of programs that are under it.

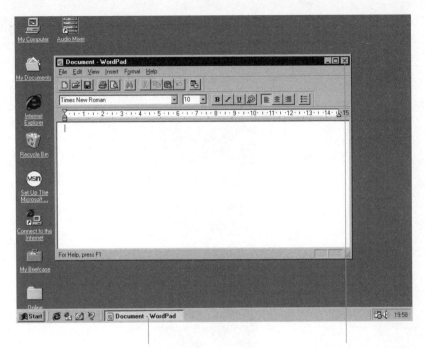

3 A button for the program appears on the Taskbar and the program starts in its own window.

4 Click on the Close button (or click on Exit under the File menu) to quit the program.

Starting a Program using Run

Your CD-ROM drive may have had a different letter assigned to it.

Windows 98 has a special 'Run' command which is usually used to run the setup program to install a new program, from say the A: floppy disk drive or the D: CD-ROM drive. However, you can use the Run command to start any other program already installed in your computer.

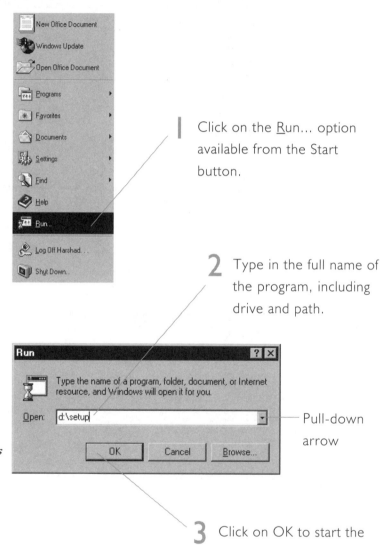

Click on the <u>R</u>un... option available from the Start button.

2 Type in the full name of the program, including drive and path.

Click on the pull-down arrow to see previous commands used. Then click on one of these commands (if appropriate) instead of typing it in.

Pull-down arrow

<u>B</u>rowse... allows you to find the program and insert the path and name in the Open box.

3 Click on OK to start the program.

Creating a Shortcut

A *Shortcut* can provide easy access to a program you use very frequently. You can place a shortcut on the desktop or in a folder.

Shortcuts can also be created to access other objects, including documents, folders, disk drives, printers, modems, faxes and even other computers.

Follow steps 1-3 to add a shortcut to a folder.
However, note that Windows will not let you create shortcuts in certain pre-supplied folders e.g. My Computer, Printers and Control Panel.

1 Drag an item onto the desktop using your right mouse button.

2 Release the mouse button to display a small menu next to the item.

If you delete a shortcut, the file that it relates to is not deleted and if you delete the file, the shortcut is not automatically deleted.

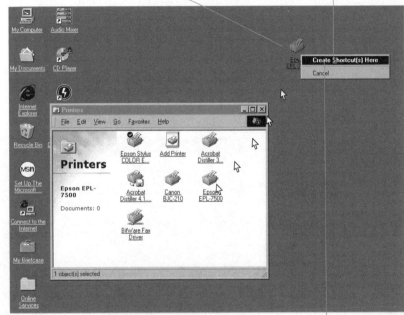

3 Click on the Create Shortcut(s) Here option. The shortcut will then appear. Note that the icon is different from the original because it has a small shortcut-arrow at the base.

Adding Start Menu Programs

The Programs menu displayed from the Start button can be changed to enter new programs or delete old entries that are no longer required. Changes you make here do not affect the actual programs stored on disk – these entries just allow you to start the programs quickly!

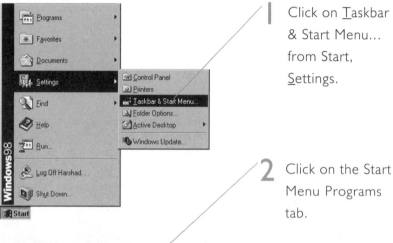

1 Click on Taskbar & Start Menu... from Start, Settings.

2 Click on the Start Menu Programs tab.

Click on the Remove... button instead of the Add... button to delete an entry from the Start Programs menu.

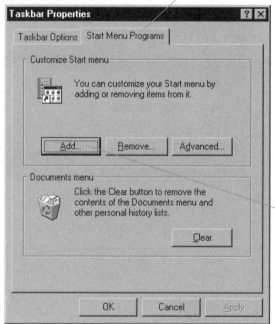

3 Click on the Add... button.

Click on the Browse... button if you don't know where the program is stored.

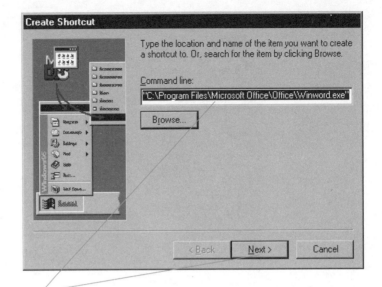

4 Type in the full name and path of the program in the Command line box and click on the Next> button.

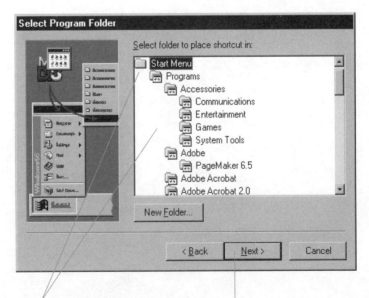

5 Select the Start Menu folder in which you want the program shortcut inserted. Click on Next.

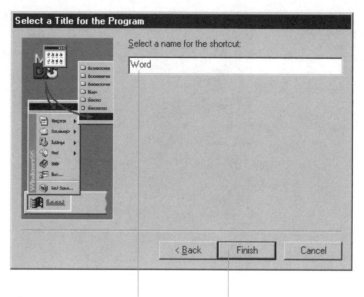

6 Type in a meaningful name for the program as you want it to appear on the Start Programs menu. Click on Finish.

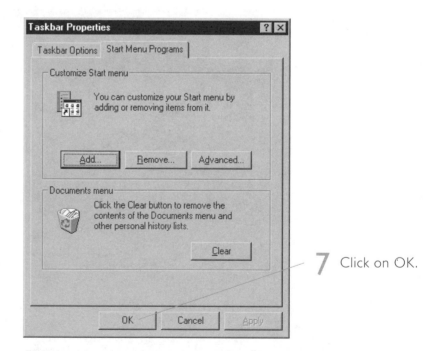

7 Click on OK.

Reorganising Start Menu Items

You can move program entries, folders and shortcuts to a new location within the Start menu.

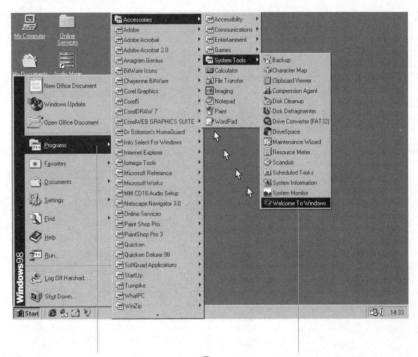

1 Click on Start and move the mouse pointer over the Programs or Favorites option.

2 Move the mouse pointer over a program, shortcut or folder you want to move. Drag it to a new location.

Using the Startup Folder

As with the previous version of Windows, the Startup feature is available in Windows 98. This allows a program or several programs to start automatically after the computer is switched on and Windows has started. Therefore, you can start work straight away on a program that you always use.

Click on Windows Explorer available from the Start button, Programs.

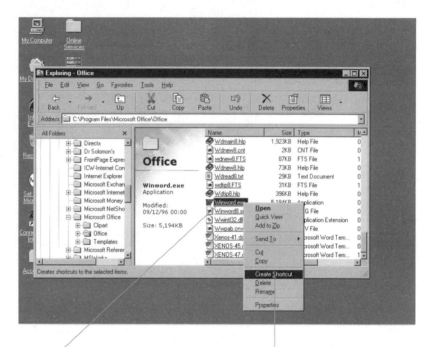

2 Find the program you want and right-click on it.

3 From the small menu displayed, click on Create Shortcut. A shortcut icon of the program selected is created.

You can use this technique to move any program to any folder.

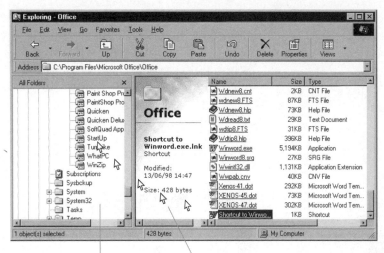

4 From the left column of folders, find the StartUp folder. To find it you may need to click on the plus sign next to the Windows folder to expand the hierarchy of folders under it, then on the Start Menu entry, and then on the Programs folder. The StartUp folder should be in this last Programs folder.

5 Drag the shortcut icon created onto the Startup folder. The program it relates to will now start automatically each time you start Windows.

Starting Programs Minimised

Sometimes you may want to start a program but not have it take over most of the desktop. You therefore need to set it up so that when it's started it is minimised automatically. When you are ready to use the program you will then only need to click on its button on the Taskbar.

1 Click on the Start button with your right mouse button and click on <u>O</u>pen from the shortcut menu displayed.

If you're currently using the Classic style (rather than Web style) view, double-click (rather than single-click) in steps 2 and 3.

(See pages 13-14 for more information on views.)

2 Click on the Programs folder from the Start Menu window displayed.

3 Click on the StartUp folder from the Programs window.

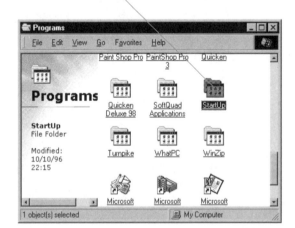

4 Select a program. Click on <u>F</u>ile and then P<u>r</u>operties from the menu.

You can also select Properties by clicking on the right mouse button after the Program is selected.

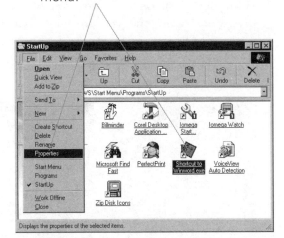

You may want several programs to start automatically when Windows starts. It is best to have them minimised, as in this example, so you can easily access them as you need to from the Taskbar.

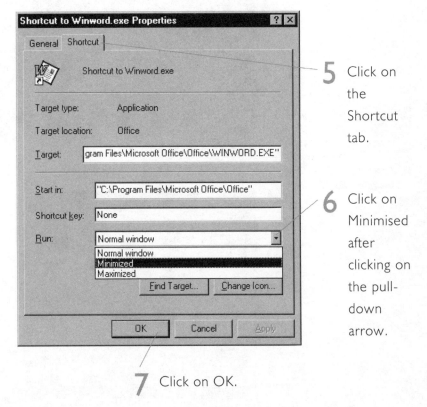

5 Click on the Shortcut tab.

6 Click on Minimised after clicking on the pull-down arrow.

7 Click on OK.

Install and Uninstall Programs

You can add (Install) new programs or just the uninstalled components of an existing program. You can also remove (Uninstall) a program – this feature is similar to that provided by the special Uninstaller utilities on the market. Note that Windows 98 can only uninstall programs specifically developed to use this feature.

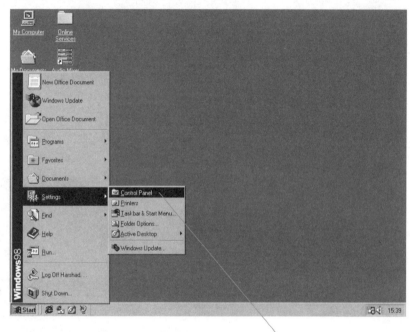

If you're currently using the Classic style (rather than Web style) view, double-click (rather than single-click) in step 2.

1 Click on Start, Settings, Control Panel.

2 Click on the Add/ Remove Programs icon.

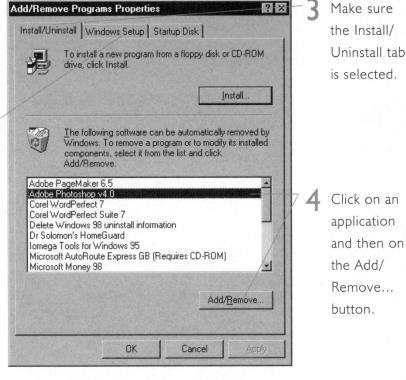

3 Make sure the Install/ Uninstall tab is selected.

Use the Windows Setup tab to Add/ Remove Windows 98 components.

4 Click on an application and then on the Add/ Remove... button.

Some programs require you to insert the original CD or floppy disks before you can continue.

5 Complete the further dialogs/messages which launch. Note the following:

• Some programs launch a tailor-made uninstall routine – simply follow the on-screen instructions.

• Other programs produce this message:

You may have to restart Windows when installation or uninstallation is complete.

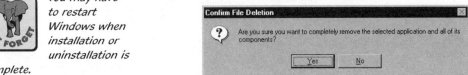

Click on Yes above and follow any further instructions.

Cut, Copy and Paste

You can move or copy information (text, graphics, etc.) from one Windows program to another, or within the same program, through a temporary storage area called the clipboard.

You can also use Cut, Copy and Paste from the Edit menu.

Press the Print Screen key on your keyboard to copy your screen display to the clipboard.

If you cut or copy another object, the previous one will be lost. Switching off has the same effect.

You can save the contents of the clipboard by choosing the Clipboard Viewer program from Accessories, System Tools.

1 Start a Program, say Paint, and select an area.

2 Right-click and select Copy from the menu displayed to copy the selection to the clipboard (Cut is the same but deletes the selection, too).

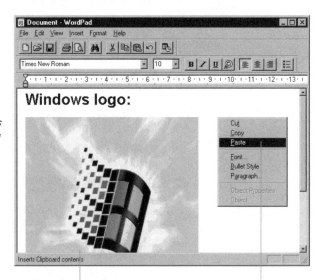

3 Start another program, say WordPad.

4 Right-click and select Paste to insert the clipboard contents.

Saving your Work

Whichever program you work with, at some stage you will need to save your work (letter, spreadsheet, drawing, etc.) as a file. There are two types of saves: changes to an existing file (Save), and saving a new file created for the first time (Save As).

Just click on Save to save the changes to an existing named file.

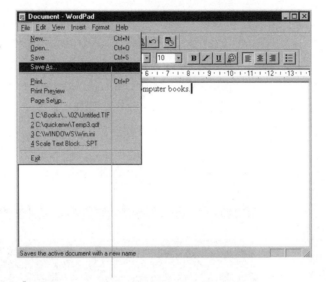

From the File menu, click on Save As...

Use Save As to copy a file by giving it another name/ location.

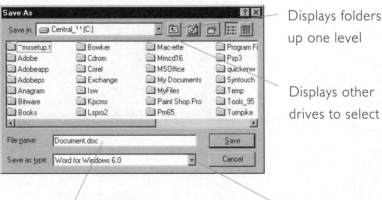

Displays folders up one level

Displays other drives to select

2 Type in a name here for your new file and click on the Save button.

Displays other file types you can save in

Running MS-DOS Applications

You can still run older MS-DOS programs (including games) in Windows 98. In fact, features like variable-size windows and scroll bars, copy and paste between Windows applications, different size TrueType fonts, etc. makes MS-DOS simply easier to control through Windows 98.

| From the Start button, select <u>P</u>rograms and then MS-DOS Prompt. The MS-DOS Prompt window displayed is like any other window, including title bar, control buttons (minimise, maximise, close), scroll bars, resize capability. A button is even inserted on the Taskbar. You can work with MS-DOS and Windows applications at the same time.

Press Alt+Enter to make the MS-DOS Prompt window full-screen if it is windowed, or vice versa.

Font/size Mark Copy Paste Full-screen   Close

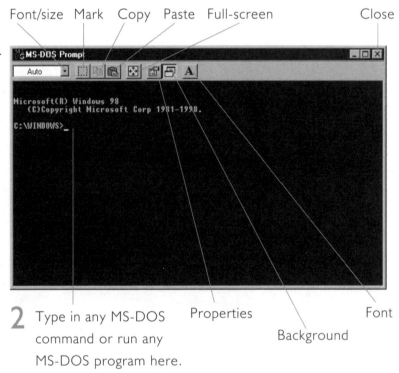

2 Type in any MS-DOS command or run any MS-DOS program here.

Properties   Font

Background

3 Click on the Close button (or type Exit and press Enter) to close the MS-DOS Prompt window.

Accessing Information

In Windows 98, the means of accessing or browsing local information (on your computer) and external information (on the Internet/network) is the same.

Covers

Chapter Four

My Computer

One way to look for all your files, regardless of where they are stored, involves using My Computer, usually located on the top left corner of the desktop.

My Computer

| Click on this icon.

If you're currently using the Classic style (rather than Web style) view, double-click (rather than single-click) in steps 1-2. (See pages 13-14 for more information on views.)

Files on a removable drive

Your PC may not have a removable drive attached to it.

Files in your 3.5" floppy disk drive

Files in your main hard disk C:

Files in your CD-ROM drive

2 Click on the appropriate drive icon from the My Computer window.

...cont'd

A file is a basic unit of storage. All your programs and documents are stored as files.

Folder

File

A Folder is the same as the older term, directory. It is used to host files.

If you're currently using the Classic style (rather than Web style) view, double-click (rather than single-click) in step 3.

3 Click on a folder to display files it contains or other folders.

You'll notice that a standard Windows file icon,

is used if the file is not associated with a specific application. Examples of files that are associated with applications and therefore have their unique icons to identify them include:

Word

Paint

WordPad

Windows Explorer

Another way to look at your files is to use Windows Explorer.

Starting Windows Explorer

Right-click on the Start button and click on Explore in the shortcut menu for a faster start.

Also right-click on other icons from the desktop, or on a folder, and then click on Explore to start Explorer showing the contents of the item chosen. Note, however, that this technique does not work with shortcut icons.

1 Click on the Start button.

2 Move pointer over Programs.

3 Click Windows Explorer.

Other ways of starting Windows Explorer

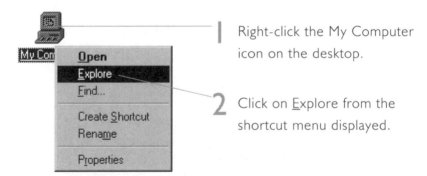

1 Right-click the My Computer icon on the desktop.

2 Click on Explore from the shortcut menu displayed.

...cont'd

If you're currently using the Classic style (rather than Web style) view, click (rather than point) in step 1.

This technique shows the contents of the selected folder in Explorer.

Or:

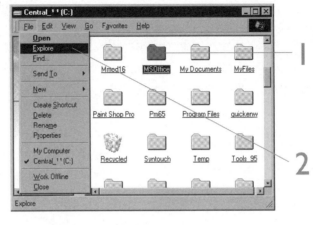

| Point to a folder until it's highlighted (few seconds).

2 Click on the File menu and then Explore.

Windows Explorer display

When you make any changes in Explorer, remember to press F5 to refresh the display.

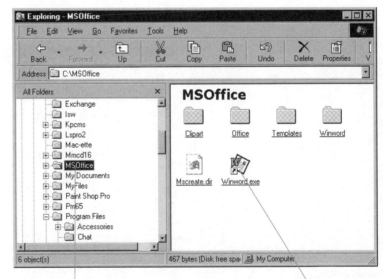

If you're currently using the Classic style (rather than Web style) view, double-click (rather than single-click) in step 2 on the right.

| Click on a folder you want to see the contents of. Folders and the files they contain are displayed on the right side.

2 Click a program icon to start it, or a document/ folder icon to open it.

See page 109 for how this technique works with the new Internet Explorer entry in the left pane.

The main benefit of using Windows Explorer instead of My Computer is that it displays a structured hierarchy of all your drives and folders on the left. Click on a plus sign next to a folder to see other folders it contains, and on a minus sign to hide this detail.

Expand folder

Collapse folder

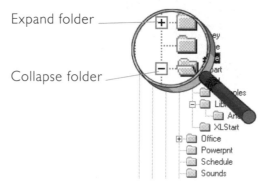

Altering the split between panes

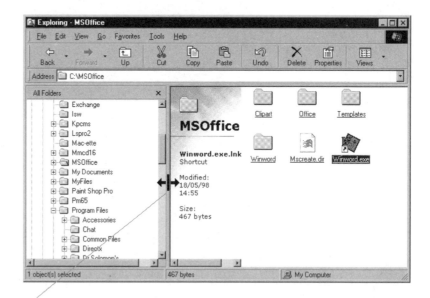

| Move the mouse pointer over the border so that it becomes double-headed.

2 Drag the border towards left or right, as appropriate.

Changing the Display

Whether you are using Windows Explorer or displaying files using My Computer, you can change the display of files by using the View menu.

1 Click on the <u>V</u>iew menu option.

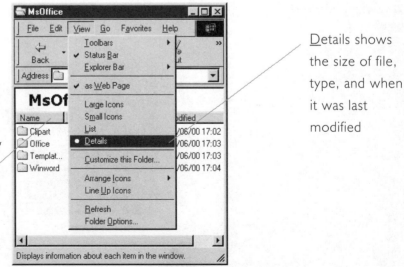

2 Click on one of the display options.

An example...

Click on any column heading to sort the list by that field, or click on it again to sort it in reverse order.

<u>D</u>etails shows the size of file, type, and when it was last modified

Active Desktop

In Windows 98 you can turn your Desktop to display 'active content' – this is content from the web that keeps changing rather than displaying a static wallpaper or background. Examples include stock ticker (to constantly keep up-to-date with stock prices), headline news, travel and weather information, to name but a few. You can add items from the Active Desktop Gallery, your favourite web sites/channels or even your own web site.

1 Right-click on the Desktop and move your mouse pointer on Active Desktop. Then select Customise my Desktop...

2 From the Web tab ensure that 'View my Active Desktop as a web page' is ticked.

3 Click on the New... button. If you want to download an item from the Active Desktop Gallery, click Yes. Alternatively, if you want to add from any other web site, click on No and type in the web address or use the Browse feature to locate the site.

Shortcut: Right-click a link in any web page and drag it to your desktop. Then click 'Create Active Desktop item(s) Here'.

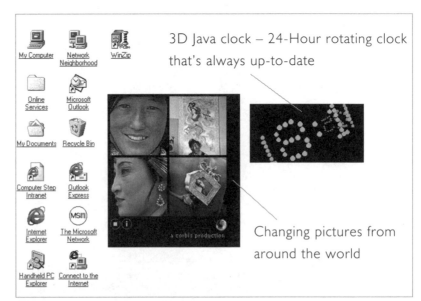

3D Java clock – 24-Hour rotating clock that's always up-to-date

Changing pictures from around the world

The Standard Buttons Toolbar

Launching

Windows 98 provides three toolbars:

Click on Toolbars, Standard Buttons from the View menu so that it is activated and ticked.

• *Standard Buttons*

• *Address Bar*

• *Links*

found in Windows Explorer, My Computer and other folders.

There are other toolbars, displayed on the Taskbar — see page 66.

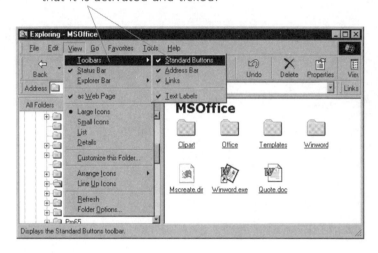

Using

 Displays previous/next folder views, or click on the arrow to select a view from the list

Shortcut key: Press Backspace to see the higher level folder/drive.

 Go one level up to a higher folder/drive

 Cut, Copy and Paste a file or a folder

 Undo last operation

Delete a file/folder

Launches the Properties dialog

The Standard toolbar buttons are automatically replaced by Internet browser ones if you access Internet Explorer.

Change the display of files/folders (click on the arrow and select a view in the menu, or click on the icon until the correct view launches)

The Address Toolbar

Launching

| Click on <u>T</u>oolbars, <u>A</u>ddress Bar from the <u>V</u>iew menu so that it is activated and ticked.

The Address Bar allows you to select and display contents from the main drives and folders in your system as well as from the Internet.

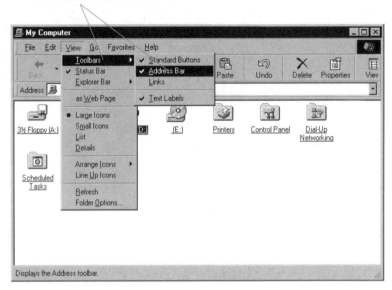

Using

You can type in any Internet web address here (or URL) to access it. Then press the Enter key. Alternatively, select the Internet Explorer entry.

2 Click on an address to have it display.

| Click on the down-arrow.

The Links Toolbar

Launching

The Links toolbar provides shortcuts to major World Wide Web sites (you don't have to pre-load your browser).

Click on Toolbars, Links from the View menu so that it is activated and ticked.

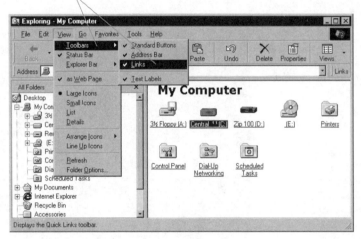

Using

To use the Links toolbar, you must have a live Internet connection.

Click on a Web address.

Switching between the Standard Buttons, Address and Links toolbars

Double-click to fully display or drag above/below/on other toolbars.

Drag vertical bar to control how much of a toolbar shows when it shares space with another.

Displaying New Toolbars

New toolbars appear on the Taskbar. To make one visible:

There are two further preset toolbars which can only display on the Taskbar (by default) or the desktop itself:

• *Quick Launch*

• *Desktop*

Use Quick Launch to access often-used features e.g: Show Desktop and Launch Outlook Express.

Use Desktop to access all of your shortcuts, in one convenient place.

2 Click on <u>T</u>oolbars. Then click on the relevant toolbar.

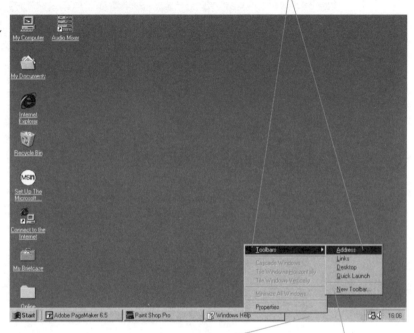

| Right-click on a blank section of the Taskbar.

Click here to create your own toolbars based on the contents of any drives/folders (including web sites)

Use the techniques shown here to make the Quick Launch and Desktop toolbars visible.

The Taskbar showing the Address toolbar

Repositioning Toolbars

You can reposition toolbars on the desktop itself:

If you want to return a toolbar to the Taskbar, simply drag it there.

2 Release the mouse button to confirm the move.

To resize/move a toolbar on the Taskbar, drag the vertical bar:

Drag here to the left or right

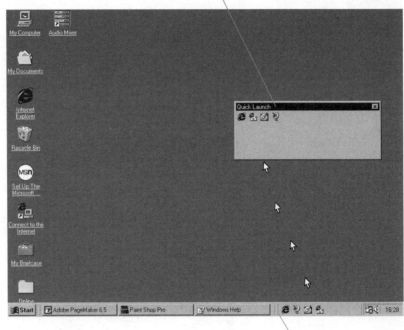

Drag a toolbar onto the desktop.

Use standard techniques to resize/reposition toolbars on the desktop.

In the above example, the Quick Launch toolbar is being relocated onto the desktop.

Extending the Quick Launch toolbar

You can drag any shortcuts you create on the desktop (see page 41) to the Quick Launch toolbar for fast easy access.

e.g. Windows Explorer in the taskbar can be launched from anywhere

Browsing with a Single Window

When using My Computer, sometimes you will need to open several folders before you reach the one that contains the file you need. You may find that each folder you activate opens a window; if this is the case, your desktop will soon be cluttered with windows you don't need.

The procedures here show you how to have additional My Computer folders open in the same window.

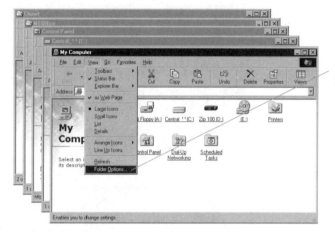

Click on the <u>V</u>iew menu and then Folder <u>O</u>ptions...

On the other hand, having separate windows for each folder is useful if you need to move or copy files between the open folders.

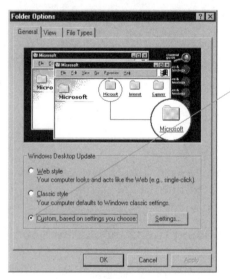

2 From the General tab, click on C<u>u</u>stom, based on settings you choose. Then click on the <u>S</u>ettings button.

3 In the Custom Settings dialog, ensure 'Open each folder in the same window' is selected, then click on OK.

Quick View

This feature allows you to look at a document without opening it or starting the program that created it. You don't even have to have the program installed on your computer!

Quick View has to be installed as an accessory in Windows 98, and can't be used for documents created using an uncommon program.

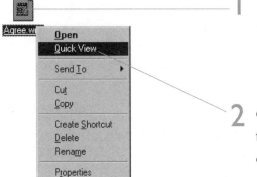

Open
Quick View

Send To ▶

Cut
Copy

Create Shortcut
Delete
Rename

Properties

| Right-click on a document icon.

2 Click on Quick View from the short menu displayed.

To close the Quick View window, press Alt+F4 when it's active.

Agree.wmf - Quick View
File   View   Help

Display details may be inaccurate.

File Naming

Up until Windows 95, long filenames such as those on the Apple Macintosh were not possible on the PC. Now, however, filenames can be up to 255 characters. Therefore you can be more descriptive when naming your files instead of being confined to just 8 characters, and 3 for the file type or extension.

Bank Manager Overdraft Request Letter ———————— Example of a long filename

When you rename a file, any hidden extension remains unchanged.

If you want, you can hide file extensions (they're still used to maintain backward compatibility with older 16-bit applications and MS-DOS), as above. To hide file extensions:

From any folder, click on Folder Options... from the View menu.

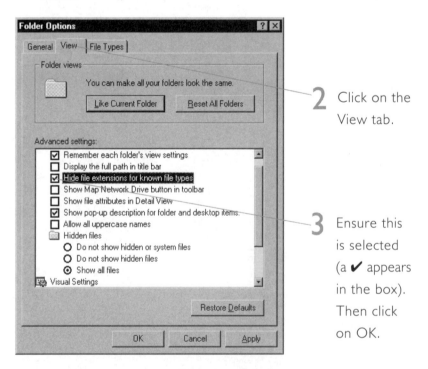

2 Click on the View tab.

3 Ensure this is selected (a ✔ appears in the box). Then click on OK.

Hidden Files

You will not normally see all the files that exist in your computer. The reason – some are deliberately hidden from view in case you accidentally change them or delete them. These important files usually help Windows and other applications/devices to work properly. They are best left hidden. However, if you need to view them:

| From any folder, click on Folder Options... from the View menu.

To return hidden and system files to their hidden status, select 'Do not show hidden or system files'.

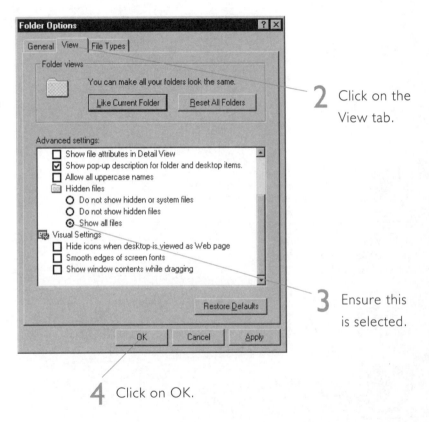

2 Click on the View tab.

3 Ensure this is selected.

4 Click on OK.

Opening Documents

Windows 98 offers several ways of opening your documents and the programs that created them without having to first start the program and then to open the document from within the program.

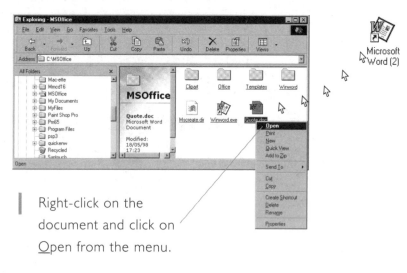

1 Right-click on the document and click on Open from the menu.

If you're currently using the Classic style (rather than Web style) view, click on the document icon (rather than move the pointer over it) in step 2.

or

2 Move the mouse pointer over the document and choose Open from the File menu at the top.

or

3 Just click on the document icon.

If you're currently using the Classic style (rather than Web style) view, double-click (rather than single-click) in step 3.

or

4 Drag the document icon onto the Program icon, either on the desktop or a folder.

or

5 Drag the document icon over the Taskbar program button. When the Program window opens, drag the icon into it; only then release the mouse button.

Working on Recent Documents

For rapid access to My Documents folder, click here:

Quite often, you'll want to open a document you have been working on recently. Windows stores details of the 15 most recent documents you have been using under <u>D</u>ocuments from the Start button, to give you fast access to them.

You can also access the 'My Documents' folder from the Desktop:

My Documents

or from the left pane of Windows Explorer:

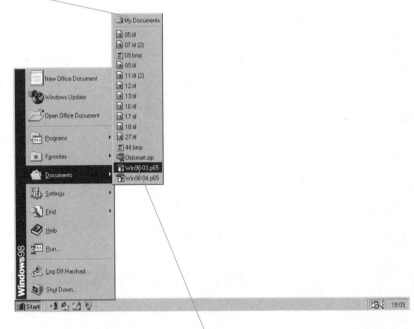

- My Documents
- Internet Explore
- Recycle Bin
- Accessories
- My Briefcase
- Online Services

Click on the required document from this list.

You can clear the display of these documents by selecting Settings, Taskbar & Start Menu..., Start Menu Programs tab, and clicking on the Clear button.
Finally, click on OK.

File Properties

Every item – file, program, shortcut, device – has Properties. You can access the Properties dialog box for all in the same way. The purpose is twofold:

- to display basic information about the item

- to change settings for the item

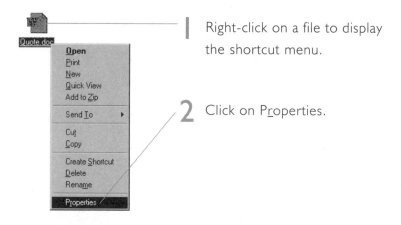

Right-click on a file to display the shortcut menu.

2 Click on Properties.

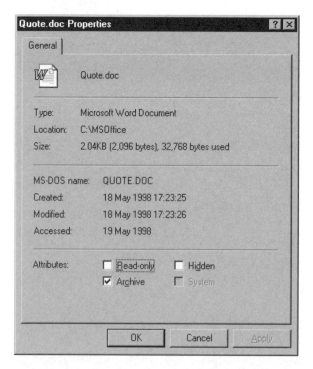

Managing Files and Folders

Remember that Folders are just logical names where files are stored. Windows handles operations on Files and Folders (like moving, copying, deleting, etc.) in a similar way and so they are both covered together here.

Covers

Chapter Five

Selecting Multiple Files/Folders

If you're currently using the Classic style (rather than Web style) view, click on a single file or folder to select it.

To select a single file or folder you simply move the mouse pointer over it to highlight it. Then you can move, copy or delete it (see the next topic). However, if you want to perform these operations on several files or folders you'll need to select all of them, so that they can then be manipulated efficiently, in one fell swoop.

Adjacent block of files

To de-select all files, click once anywhere outside the selection area.

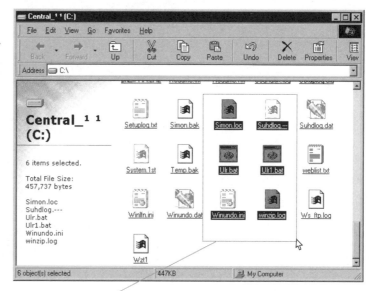

Selecting files here can include whole folders, which may contain other files.

| Drag out a box to cover all the files you want selected.

or

Step 2 – if you're currently using the Classic style (rather than Web style) view, hold down one SHIFT key. Then click on the first and last items in the group.

2 Point to the first item for a few seconds until it's highlighted. Then press and hold down one SHIFT key and point to the last item in the group until the whole group is highlighted, indicating that it's selected.

Non-adjacent files

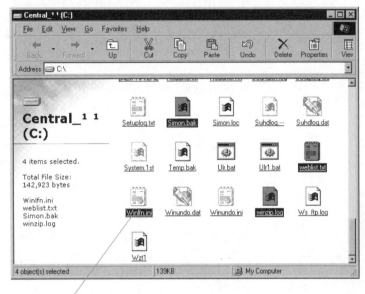

To de-select a file, either Ctrl+point (web view) or Ctrl+click (classic view) on it again.

Step 1 – if you're currently using the Classic style (rather than Web style) view, hold down the Ctrl key. Then click on the individual items.

To select several non-adjacent files, press and hold down the Ctrl key. Then point to as many files as required (until they're highlighted).

To select all files (and folders) in a window, click on Select All from the Edit menu.

Press Ctrl+A to select all files and folders in the active window.

Copying and Moving Files/Folders

You may want to copy/move a file to the same disk (a different folder) or to another (e.g. a floppy) disk. There are several ways you can achieve this. For speed and simplicity, however, the first method – using the right mouse button – is recommended.

Using the right mouse button

1 Start Windows Explorer. In the window on the left, select the folder that contains the file you want to copy or move.

2 In the window on the right, select the file you want to copy or move.

Instead of a single file you can copy/move multiple files (just select as shown in the last topic), or copy/move a folder using the same technique.

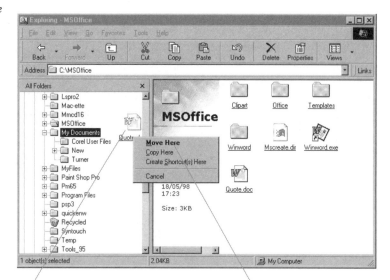

3 Using the right mouse button drag the file you want to copy/move onto the destination folder or drive (in the window on the left) so that it is highlighted. Then release to display a shortcut menu.

4 Click on the Move Here or Copy Here option.

Using the left mouse button

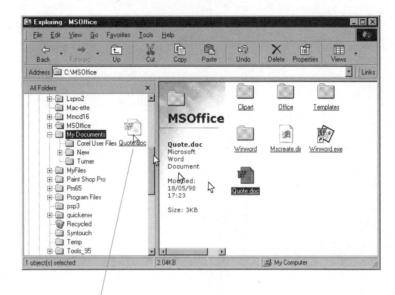

| Using the left mouse button drag a file (or multiple files/ folders) to the destination folder or drive in the window on the left.

2 To move/copy files to the same drive or to another drive, follow this simple technique:

You'll notice a little '+' symbol in a box if the file is going to be copied. Otherwise, the file will be moved.

Copy to another drive	*Just drag*
Move to another drive	*Hold down the Shift key when dragging*
Copy to same drive	*Hold down the Ctrl key when dragging*
Move to same drive	*Just drag*

Using Cut, Copy, Paste

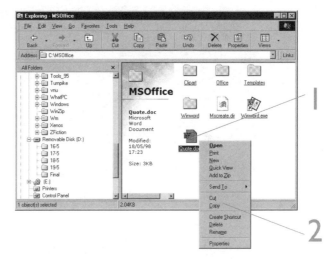

I   Right-click on a file.

2   From the shortcut menu click on Cut (to move) or Copy.

3   Open a window for the folder you want to copy/move the file into. Then right-click the mouse button in a blank area of the window.

You can also use Cut, Copy and Paste from the Edit menu.

4   Click on Paste from the shortcut menu.

Explicitly to a Floppy disk

Make sure there is a floppy disk in your drive before copying or moving files to it.

1 Right-click on a file.

2 Move the pointer over Send To.

3 Click here to copy the file to a floppy disk.

Keep the Shift key pressed when selecting the floppy disk to Move the file instead of Copying it.

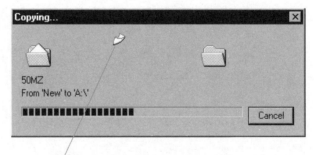

An animation of a file flying across is shown whenever a file (or group of files) is moved, copied or deleted.

Deleting Files/Folders

Deleting files and folders is easy and safe in Windows 98 (see the next topic, Recycle Bin, too). Note that you can delete a file from wherever it is listed, although the My Computer display is shown here.

You can press the Delete key on your keyboard instead of selecting Delete from the menu.

Delete can also be chosen by right-clicking on the file and selecting it from the shortcut menu displayed.

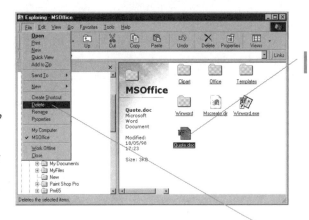

Select one or more files/folders (see earlier topic).

2 Click on Delete from the File menu.

You can also delete a file by dragging it onto the Recycle Bin icon on the desktop.

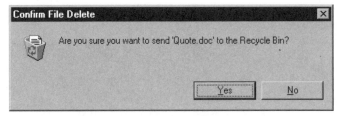

3 Click on Yes above.

If you suddenly realise that you have made a mistake deleting one or more files, choose Undo Delete from the Edit menu straightaway. Alternatively, use the Recycle Bin to retrieve it (see next topic).

The Recycle Bin

Files that you delete from your floppy disk or from the MS-DOS command prompt don't go into the Recycle Bin.

The Recycle Bin is a place where deleted files are kept. They are not physically deleted from your hard disk until you 'empty' the Recycle Bin (or erase them within the Bin itself). The Recycle Bin therefore provides a safety net for files you may delete by mistake and allows you to easily retrieve them.

A drawback of the Recycle Bin is that from time to time, you'll have to empty it to free up disk space taken up by deleted files.

If you're currently using the Classic style (rather than Web style) view, double-click (rather than single-click) in step 1.

Restoring files

Recycle Bin

1 | Click on the Recycle Bin icon from the desktop.

You can also restore folders.

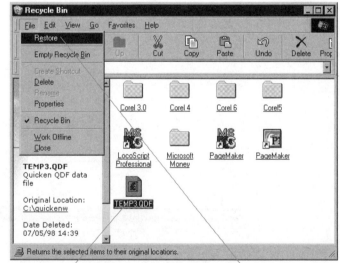

To make it easier to find the file, you can display this list by Name, Origin, Delete Date, Type or Size. These options are all available from the View menu, Arrange Icons.

2 Select a file you want to restore, or multiple files (using the techniques described on pages 76–77).

3 Click on Restore from the File menu to rescue the file(s) back to the original location.

If you're currently using the Classic style (rather than Web style) view, double-click (rather than single-click) in step 1.

Emptying the Recycle Bin

Recycle Bin

1 Click on the Recycle Bin icon from the desktop.

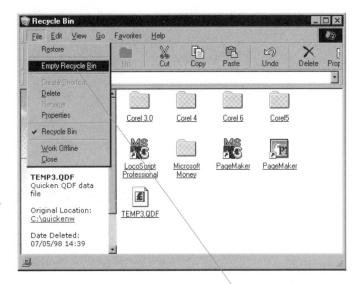

If you only want to erase certain files in the Bin, select them. Omit steps 2-3. Instead, click on Delete in the File menu. In the Confirm File Delete dialog, click on Yes.

2 Click on Empty Recycle Bin from the File menu to reclaim lost disk space.

3 Click on Yes above.

Bypassing the Recycle Bin globally

*Be very careful
about which
files you delete
using these
techniques.*

If you want, you can have Windows 98 *permanently* erase files
or folders when you delete them – in other words, they
aren't copied to the Recycle Bin.

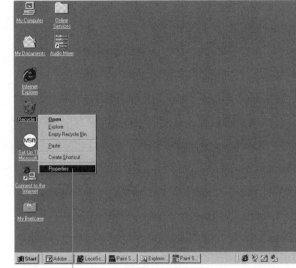

*You can use a
special
technique
which lets you
specify that
individual deletions bypass
the Recycle Bin.*

*Don't follow steps 1–2.
Instead, select the file/
folder(s) you want to delete,
then simply hold down one
SHIFT key as you press the
Delete key.*

*Finally, in the Confirm File
Delete dialog, click on Yes.*

Right-click on the Recycle Bin icon. Then click Properties.

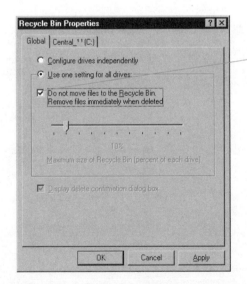

2 Click here (a ✔
appears). Then
click on OK.

Creating a New File/Folder

You can create new files in standard formats for use with specific programs installed on your computer. Also using the same option, you can create new folders to organise your files into.

The New option to create a file/ folder is also accessible from the desktop. Just right-click the mouse button.

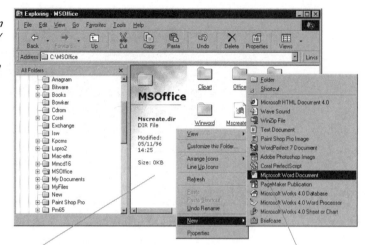

1 | Open a folder (from My Computer or Windows Explorer) you want to create a file or folder in.

2 | Right-click. Move the pointer over New, and then click on Folder to create a new folder. To create a file click on one of the file formats in the bottom section of the menu.

3 | Type a name for the file/ folder created and then press the ENTER key.

Renaming a File/Folder

You can rename a file/folder at any time. It is done very easily too, by simply editing the current name.

Use the same method to rename icons on the desktop. You won't be able to rename the Recycle Bin, though!

| Right-click on a file/folder. Then click on Rename in the shortcut menu.

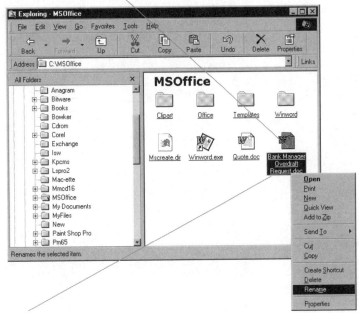

2 The current name will be boxed in heavier line. Type the new name, or use the cursor arrow keys to position the cursor and edit only part of the name.

3 Press the ENTER key or click your mouse pointer outside the file name to confirm the new name.

Backtracking File Operations

If you accidentally delete, rename, copy or move a file, you can undo (reverse) the operation. Furthermore, you can even undo several preceding operations instead of just the last one (multi-level undo feature).

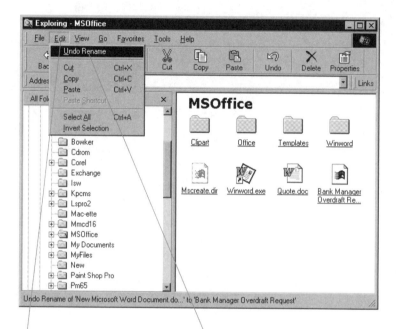

1 Click on Edit from any folder. At the top of the menu which appears, an Undo of the last file operation is displayed.

2 Click on the Undo operation. Repeat, if you need to undo any more operations.

Finding Lost Files/Folders

The Find feature in Windows 98 is very powerful. The search can be based on partial file names, specific dates, given file types/sizes or text within the files. Once the desired files are found you can open them or perform other operations (including deleting, renaming, copying, displaying properties, etc.) – all from the search results displayed without going into Windows Explorer!

For more advanced searches, see page 90.

The On the Internet... and People options relate to Internet searches – see chapter 7 for more information on using the Internet.

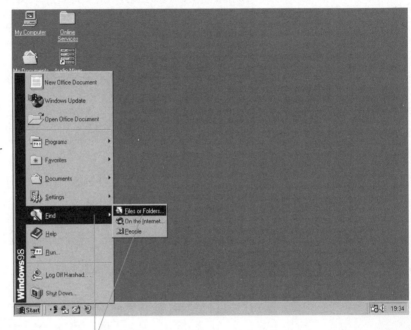

To search for text within files, type in the search text here:

Point to Find from the Start button and click on Files or Folders...

To limit the search to specific drives, select it here:

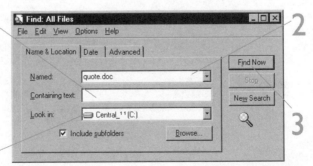

2 Click and then type in full/part name of the file or folder.

3 Click to start the search.

Advanced techniques: searches by date range

To find files within a specific date range:

1 Click on the Date tab. Then Find all files, followed by Modified, Created or Last accessed.

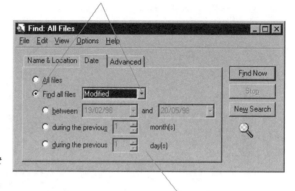

The actions described here are optional, and supplement the basic search procedures described on page 89. Carry out the steps here before you perform step 3 on page 89.

2 Complete the parameter fields.

Advanced techniques: searches by file type/size

To find files of a specific type or size:

1 Click on the arrow. In the list, select a file type (e.g. Backup File for Microsoft Backup).

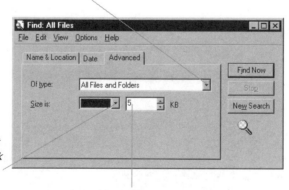

To further limit the search, click on this arrow: and select At least or At most.

2 Type in a file size (in kilobytes).

Acting on search results

When a search has been completed, this is the result:

 When you've finished using the Find dialog, press Alt+F4 to close it.

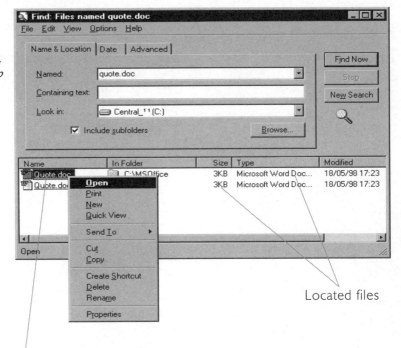

Located files

Right-click on a file. Then click on <u>O</u>pen to edit the file in the program associated with it; <u>D</u>elete to erase it; Rena<u>m</u>e to amend the file's title; <u>C</u>opy to copy the file; Cu<u>t</u> to copy and delete it; or P<u>r</u>operties to view/alter the related properties.

Creating Scraps

A 'scrap' is a piece of text copied/moved into a folder or onto the desktop, so that it can be used somewhere else by a simple drag operation. This technique serves the same purpose as the Cut, Copy and Paste operations described in Chapter 3, but it is more intuitive.

 Keep the Shift key pressed when dragging the text block out to Move it instead of Copying.

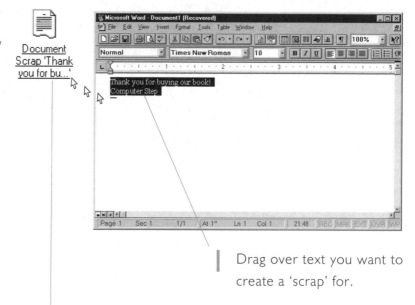

Document Scrap 'Thank you for bu...'

Drag over text you want to create a 'scrap' for.

2 Drag the block of text onto the desktop or into a folder.

 Drag the Document Scrap icon onto the Recycle Bin icon to delete it, when no longer required.

3 Drag the newly created Document Scrap into another document as required and its contents will be copied there.

Outlook Express

Use Outlook Express to send and receive e-mail (providing you have an Internet connection). You can also use it to maintain a comprehensive contact database.

Covers

Chapter Six

Starting Outlook Express

Mail you receive is stored in the Inbox. Mail waiting to be sent is stored in the Outbox. Mail which has been despatched is to be found in the Sent Items folder. Messages you've deleted are kept in the Deleted Items folder.

You can use Outlook Express to:

- send e-mail

- receive e-mail

- maintain a comprehensive contact database

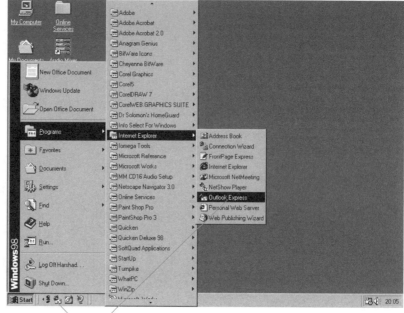

Click on Hang Up in the File menu when you want to close your connection, or select to do this automatically from the Dial Up tab in Tools, Options... to avoid unnecessarily paying for online charges.

Outlook Express

Click on Start, Programs, Internet Explorer. Then click on Outlook Express. Alternatively, select it from the desktop shortcut icon or the Quick Launch icon on the taskbar.

If you don't want Outlook Express to prompt you to connect to the Internet everytime you start it, select 'Do not dial a connection' in the Dial Up tab within Tools, Options... Alternatively, you can select to log on to your service provider automatically, once you've set up an account and run the Internet Connection wizard (see next topic).

Setting up Accounts

Before you can use Outlook Express to send and receive e-mail, you must:

A.   set up a mail account

B.   run the Internet Connection wizard

C.   connect to your service provider (if you didn't do this when you started Outlook Express)

Step A leads automatically to step B and only needs to be done once initially. Step C has to be carried out every time before you can send/receive e-mail.

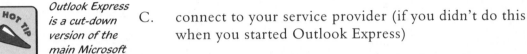

Outlook Express is a cut-down version of the main Microsoft Outlook product. Detailed coverage of both is in the book, Outlook 2000 in easy steps.

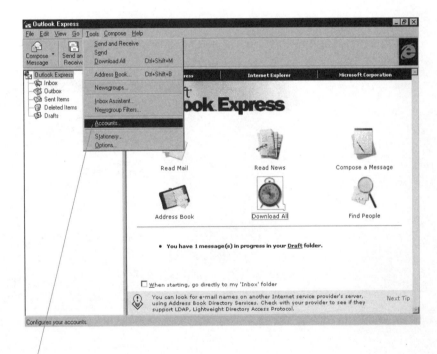

Click on Tools, then Accounts.

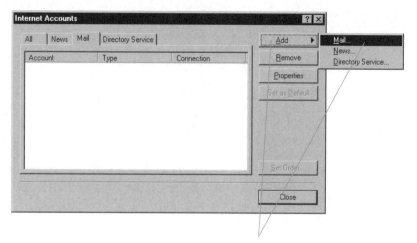

2 Click on Add, Mail...

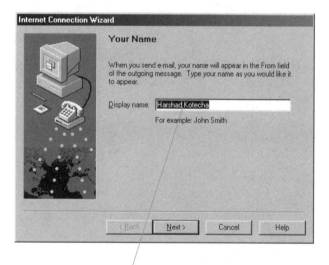

3 The Internet Connection wizard launches. Type in the name you want to appear in your e-mail. Then click on Next.

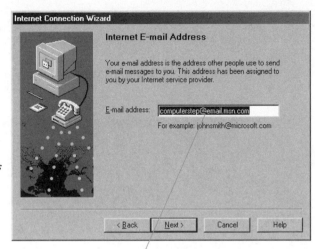

Step 5 –
Outlook Express
currently
supports these
mail servers:

• POP3

• IMAP

4 Type in your e-mail address. Then click on Next.

5 Click on the arrow, then select a mail server.

Step 6 –your
service provider
will supply this
information.

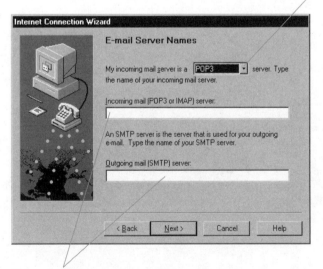

You may well
find that you'll
also have to
change TCP/IP
file protocols
(activate the Networks icon
in Control Panel, then select
TCP/IP) – your service
provider will advise.

6 Complete these fields. Then click on Next.

7 Complete the remaining dialogs until the Next box becomes
Finish. Then click on this.

Checking your Mail

Mail which is sent to you is stored by your service provider, and downloaded to you when you log on.

1 | Click on Outlook Express and then on the Connect button.

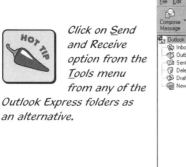

Click on Send and Receive option from the Tools menu from any of the Outlook Express folders as an alternative.

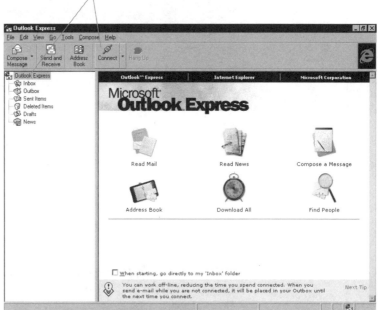

Outgoing mail is stored in the Outbox, and sent at the same time as incoming mail is delivered. It's then kept in Sent Items.

2 Confirm connection to your service provider, after checking your User Name and Password entries. This dialog varies depending on your service provider.

Reading Messages

Downloaded messages are stored in your Inbox.

Note the following icons to the left of messages:

The message is unread (note that the message entry is in bold).

The message has been read (the entry is in light type).

By default, Outlook Express marks a message as 'read' when it has been previewed for 5 seconds.

To delete a message, follow step 1. Then drag the message to the Deleted Items folder in the left pane.

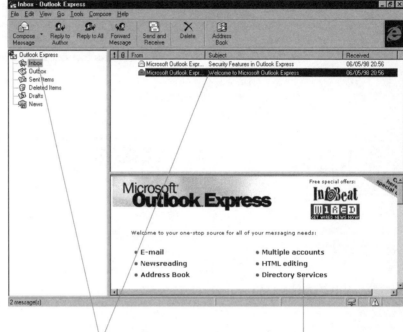

| Click on Inbox. Then click on the message you want to read.

The Preview window

2 Scroll through your message in the Preview window.

Reading mail with the special editor

This is an alternative way to read your mail.

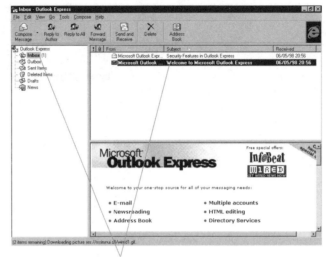

The procedures described on page 101 can also be carried out within the editor.

Click on Inbox. Then double-click on the message you want to read.

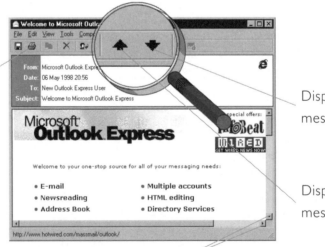

To print your message on the default printer, click on the Print button. Choose *Print...* from the *File* menu for the Print dialog box.

Displays next message

Displays previous message

2 Scroll through your message.

3 Press Alt+F4 or click on the Close button when you've finished.

Replying to a Message

Open a message in the Preview window or the special editor (see pages 99–100).

Step 2 – to send the reply to all the recipients of the message you were reading, click on the Reply to All button instead:

 2 Click on the Reply to Author button in the toolbar.

4 Click on Send button (or select Send Message from the File menu).

To attach a file to a message, click on this button:

Then select a file from the Insert Attachment dialog. Finally, click on Attach.

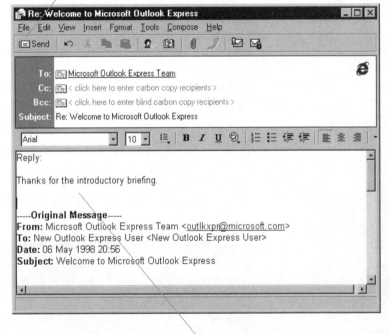

To forward a message, follow step 1. Click on the Forward Message button:

Carry out steps 3-4.

3 Type your reply here.

Batching Messages

If you have several messages to send, it's economical to batch them all together and send them with only one connection to your service provider. To batch messages in Outbox, select the Send Later option from the File menu. Then, when you're ready, send them all – see page 98.

Composing a New Message

Click on the arrow to the right of the button for a list of 'stationery' (message style) options. Click on a stationery. Then follow steps 2-4, as appropriate.

1 Click on the Compose Message button (available in any Outlook Express folder except the editor).

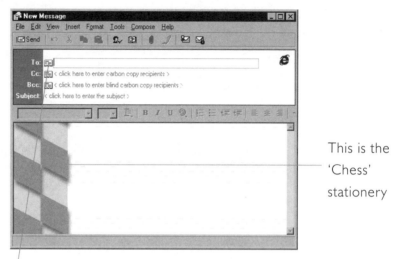

This is the 'Chess' stationery

2 Type the name of the recipient and click the Check Names button or click on (to the right of the T_o... button) to launch the Address book (and follow steps 3-4).

To launch Address Book click on this button:

Address Book

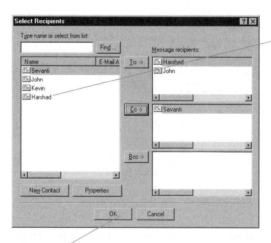

3 Select name and click on the T_o & C_c (courtesy copy) buttons. Add as many names as you want.

4 Click on OK and follow steps 3–4 on page 101.

Web Browsing and Publishing

In this chapter, you'll run the Internet Connection Wizard to prepare for using the Web. You'll use Windows 98's Dial-Up Networking feature to log on to your service provider, and then browse the Web in various ways (including from within Windows Explorer itself). Finally, you'll create your own Web pages, and then publish them to the Internet.

Covers

Chapter Seven

An Overview

Windows 98 lets you perform the following Internet-related actions. You can:

- connect to the Web directly, with or without using connection software provided by your service provider

- browse the Web directly, by launching Internet Explorer or from any folder (e.g. Windows Explorer, My Computer and Control Panel)

- create your own Web pages (with FrontPage Express)

- publish Web pages on the Web (with the Web Publishing wizard)

Internet Connection Wizard

We've already seen (in chapter 6) that creating an account in Outlook Express automatically runs the Internet Connection Wizard. If you've carried out this procedure, you shouldn't need to run the wizard now in order to use the Web (although you may need to fine-tune your settings). If you haven't, do the following:

You may well need to customise your TCP/IP settings (available from the Network folder in Control Panel).

Contact your service provider for more information.

1 Click on Start, Programs, Internet Explorer. Then click on Connection Wizard.

Right-click on the Internet Explorer icon from the desktop and choose Properties from the shortcut menu to further customise your Internet settings (or select the Internet icon from the Control Panel).

2 In the first screen, ensure the following option is selected: *I have an existing Internet account through my phone line or a local area network (LAN). Help me set up my computer to connect to this Internet account.* Click on Next.

3 Complete each remaining dialog, clicking on Next to move on to the subsequent screen.

4 When the Finish button appears, click on it.

Logging on to the Internet

To follow the procedures described here:

- *you must have run the Internet Connection Wizard at some point*
- *your modem must be switched on*

You can log on to your service provider:

- by running the relevant software supplied by your provider (if you're unsure about this, contact your provider for more information)

- by following a specific procedure within Windows 98

Logging on from Windows

Click on the My Computer icon on your desktop.

To locate people on the Web, click on Start, Find, People. In the Find People dialog, type in details of the person you want to find (e.g. name). In the Look in: field, select a directory service (e.g. WhoWhere). Click on Find Now.

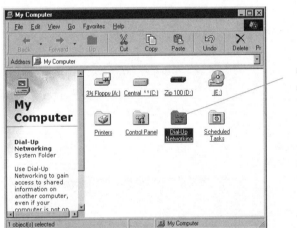

2 Click on Dial-Up Networking.

If you're currently using the Classic style (rather than Web style) view, double-click (rather than single-click) in steps 1-3.

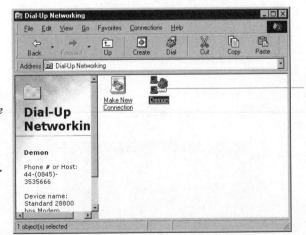

3 Click on the icon representing your service provider.

Windows remembers your password, so you only need to enter it the first time you log on.

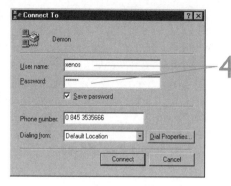

4 Type in your user (account) name, then – if applicable – your password. Then click on Connect.

Tracking progress

After step 4, Windows 98 attempts to connect to your service provider:

A failed connection produces an error message.

When the connection has been made, this message appears:

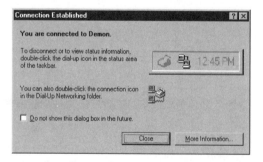

When you've finished with your connection, click on the Disconnect button. Then follow step 5.

For more details of the connection, double-click this icon – 🖥 – in the Taskbar:

5 Click on OK.

Browsing the Web

Internet access is seamlessly integrated within Windows 98. There are so many different ways you can browse the Web:

- directly, by launching and using Internet Explorer

- from within any folder

- by using the Address or Links toolbar

- from the left pane of Windows Explorer

- by using Channels/Favorites

You can also browse constantly at a Web page/item by adding it to your Active Desktop – see page 62.

Internet Explorer

Click on Start, Programs, Internet Explorer. Then click on Internet Explorer. Alternatively, start Internet Explorer from its desktop or taskbar icon.

Step 2 – instead, click on the Favorites button and select a site. See page 110 for more details.

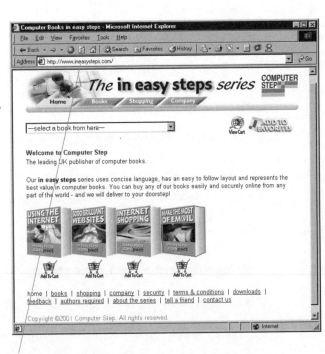

2 Type in the address of the Web site you want to visit (e.g: www.ineasysteps.com). Then press Enter.

When you type in an address, Windows tries to finish it based on sites you've visited.
In this way, typing:

www.i

(for example) is likely to insert the full ineasysteps address.

Browsing from any folder

Click on the Windows logo. It turns into a rotating globe to represent the World Wide Web. A connection dialog is launched and then you are connected to Microsoft's default web site, http://home.microsoft.com

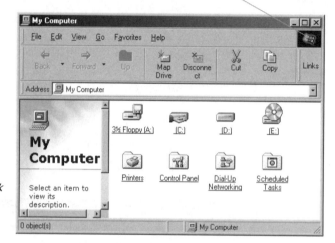

To search for Web sites, click on this button in Internet Explorer:

The Search bar launches on the left side of the screen. Type in text to search for, then click on one of the 5 search engines listed (e.g. Lycos). Click on Search. The search engine displays matches; click on one to display its site.

Browsing from the Address toolbar

Type in an address and press Enter. The Address toolbar can be activated from any folder (see page 64) or displayed on the taskbar (see page 66).

Browsing from the Links toolbar

Click on a link button. The Links toolbar can be activated from any folder (see page 65) or displayed on the taskbar (see page 66).

Browsing via Windows Explorer

You can use the new 'Internet Explorer' entry in the left pane of Windows Explorer to access the Web. Click on it to:

- automatically superimpose the Internet Explorer toolbar on top of the Standard Windows toolbar

- display web pages in the right pane of the Windows Explorer display, where contents of folders is normally displayed

To set your default Home page, click on Internet Options... in the View menu after step 2. In the Internet Options dialog, ensure the General tab is active. In the Address field, type in the relevant Home page, e.g.

http://www.ineasysteps.com

Click on OK.

1. Click on Start, Programs, Windows Explorer.

2. Click on Internet Explorer.

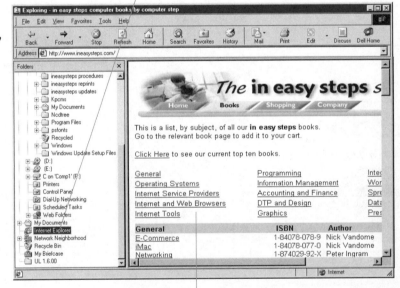

3. Your default Home page displays here.

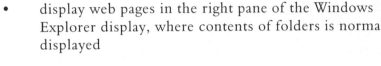

Once you're surfing the web, you'll be able to expand the Internet Explorer entry in the left pane (click on the little plus sign). This will show any current open pages (and frame sets). The last page you visited is stored here even after you've disconnected from the Internet, enabling quick access next time you connect in the current logon session.

Browsing via Favorites

Favorites are sites you've previously visited and deemed worthy of revisiting. Note that it's spelled in American rather than as 'Favourites' in English.

You can also access Favorites by another route (without having to pre-load Internet Explorer).

Click on Start, Favorites. Then click the Favorite you want to access.

1 Start the Internet Explorer Web browser, by using any of the techniques described on pages 107–109.

2 Click on Favorites.

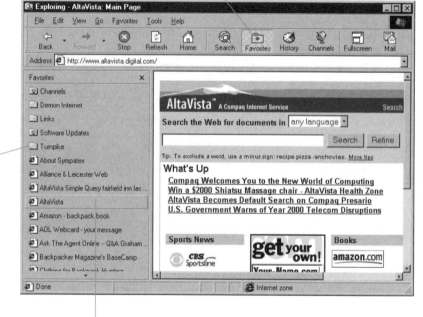

Click on a folder: for access to more entries. For instance, click on Channels to produce:

See pages 111-112 for how to use channels.

3 Click on a Favorite.

Creating Your Own Favorites

To add the current page to your list of favorites, click on Add to Favorites... in the Favorites menu. In the dialog, click on OK.

Browsing via Channels

You can also subscribe to standard Web sites (for how to subscribe to channels, see later).

To initiate a subscription, open the relevant Web page. Click on Add to Favorites... in the Favorites menu. Then, select one of the following:

• Partial subscriptions: tell me when updates occur.

• Full subscriptions: download for offline reading.

Click on OK.

A 'channel' is a special type of Web site designed to deliver content to your PC. You can view channels:

- by clicking on an entry in the Channel Bar

- directly from within Internet Explorer

- from View Channels icon on the taskbar (if Quick Launch toolbar is set – see page 66)

In practice, channels work much like any Web site, but the process of subscription is much more relevant. Subscription isn't compulsory, but it does have the advantage – if you opt for it – of ensuring that comprehensive site content is downloaded to your hard disk for off-line viewing. Alternatively, you can simply choose to be notified when the site details are updated.

Click on the View Channels icon from the taskbar OR perform step 1 below.

If the Channel Bar isn't visible, right-click on the desktop. In the shortcut menu, click Properties. In the Display Properties dialog, click on the Web tab. Select Internet Explorer Channel Bar. Click on OK.

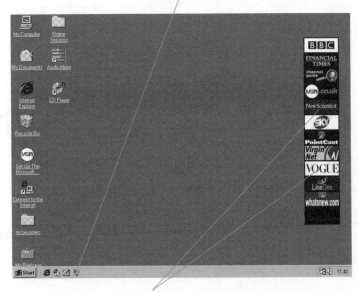

Click on a channel OR perform steps 1–4 overleaf.

...cont'd

To print a Web page, press Ctrl+P. Select the relevant print options, then click on OK.

| Click on Start, Programs, Internet Explorer, and Internet Explorer again.

To subscribe to a channel, follow steps 1-2. Click on this channel entry:

Then follow the on-screen instructions.

3 Click on a channel entry.

2 Click on the Channels button.

4 When you've finished, click on the close button or press Alt+F4 to exit from Internet Explorer.

Don't forget to terminate your Internet connection when you've finished browsing the Web.

Creating a Web Page

 FrontPage Express has a special wizard – the Personal Home Page Wizard – which you can use to create a Home Page easily and conveniently.

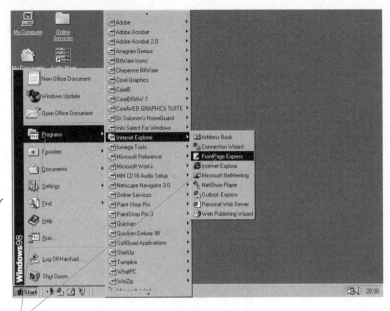

| Click on Start, Programs, Internet Explorer. Then click on FrontPage Express.

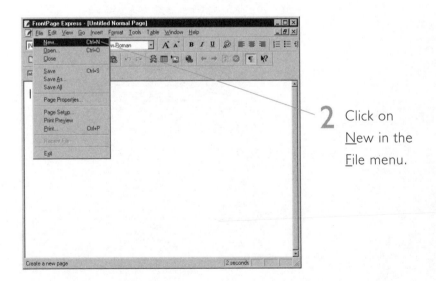

2 Click on New in the File menu.

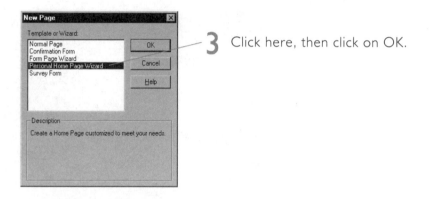

3 Click here, then click on OK.

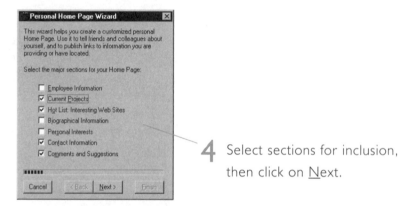

4 Select sections for inclusion, then click on Next.

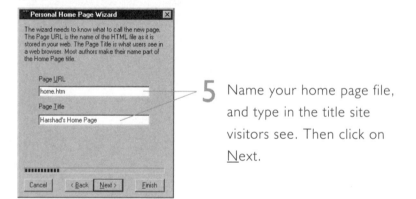

5 Name your home page file, and type in the title site visitors see. Then click on Next.

6 Complete the remaining dialogs. When the Finish button appears, click on it.

Formatting a Web Page

To realign text, select it. Click on Paragraph in the Format menu. Click on the arrow to the right of the Paragraph Alignment field, then select an alignment. Click on OK.

1 Immediately after creating a new Web page, carry out steps 2–3 below.

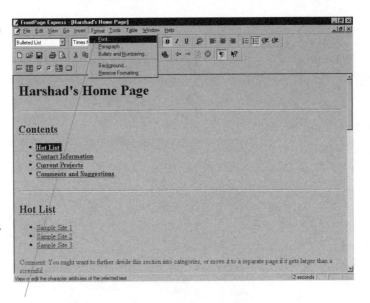

Don't forget to save your work. Click on Save As in the File menu. Click on the As File button. Select a drive/folder, type in a filename and click on Save.

2 To reformat text, select it. Click on Font... in the Format menu.

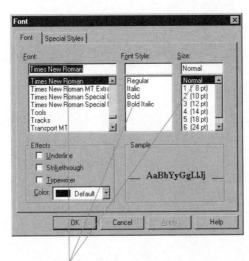

To apply a full style, click on the Special Styles tab. Select a style (e.g. Citation), then click on OK.

3 Select a font, font style and/or size. Then click on OK.

Publishing Web Pages

When you've finished creating your Web pages, you can use the Web Publishing Wizard to send them to your service provider's server, or to any other server hosting your Web site.

1 With the new Web pages still open in FrontPage Express, click on Start, Programs, Internet Explorer. Then click on Web Publishing Wizard.

To search for specific sites on the Web after you've logged on, click on Start, Find, On the Internet. Internet Explorer launches. Select a search engine on the left. Then either:

- *type in brief details of the site (e.g. ineasysteps), then click on Search*

or

- *click on a preset topic (e.g. Investing).*

2 Click on Next.

3 Complete each remaining dialog, clicking on Next to move on to the subsequent screen.

4 When the Finish button appears, click on it.

Printing

Whether you want a hard copy of documents you've created using an application (Word, Excel, etc.), or you want to print information from the Web or your e-mail messages, you'll need a printing capability.

This chapter shows you everything you need to know about printing under Windows 98.

Covers

Chapter Eight

Printer Setup

Before you set up your printer to work with Windows, ensure that it is connected to your computer and make a note of the printer manufacturer and model number.

A Network printer can be set up instead of a local one through the Add Printer wizard.

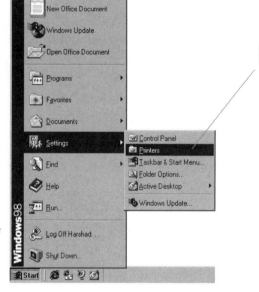

| Click on the Start button, move the pointer over Settings, and click Printers.

If you're currently using the Classic style (rather than Web style) view, double-click (rather than single-click) in step 2. (See pages 13-14 for more information on views.)

2 Click the Add Printer icon.

3 Follow the instructions on screen given by the Add Printer Wizard (see Chapter 1, Page 22). An icon for your new printer is available in the Printers folder when finished.

Fonts

All the fonts installed on your computer are usually stored in one place: C:\WINDOWS\FONTS. To access the Fonts folder, click on Start, Settings, Control Panel, Fonts.

You can manage these fonts easily by treating them as files. For example, you can add new fonts by dragging them to the Fonts folder, delete old ones by deleting them from the Fonts folder, etc... (see Chapter 5 for full details on all File operations).

Another useful feature is that you can preview any font before you decide to use it:

 Change the display for further information about fonts.

For instance, if you click on the List Fonts By Similarity option from the View menu, and then use the List fonts by similarity to: field to select a base font – Windows tells you which fonts resemble it.

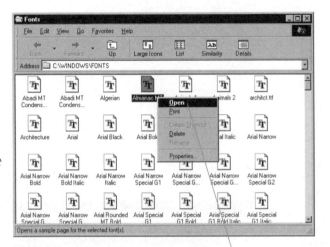

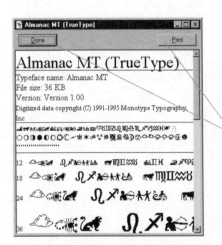

1 Right-click on the font you want to preview, then click on Open in the shortcut menu.

2 A preview of the selected font is displayed. Click on Print to get a printout of it, or just click Done.

Printing Documents

Once your printer is set up in Windows, printing is easy.
You can print a document from the Program that created it
or by dragging the file onto the Printer icon.

From the menu

Click on this icon:

in the toolbar to quickly print one copy of the whole document to the default printer set up, and thus avoid the Print dialog box altogether.

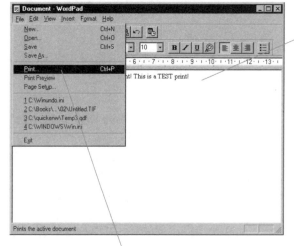

Type in some text in your application, or open a document you want to print.

2 Click on File and then Print...

You can use a keyboard shortcut to launch the Print dialog: simply press Ctrl+P.

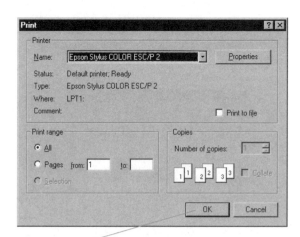

3 Click on OK after amending the options, if required (e.g. pages to print, no. of copies).

Using drag-and-drop

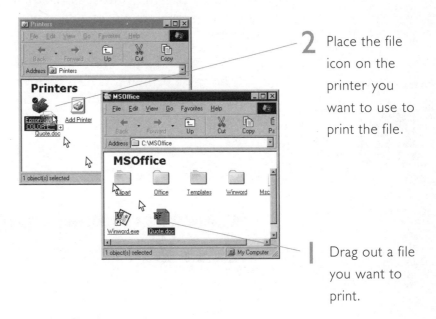

2 Place the file icon on the printer you want to use to print the file.

Drag out a file you want to print.

You can have a shortcut icon for a specific printer rather than the actual printer icon – if you are going to use the drag-and-drop technique often, create a shortcut icon for your main printer on the desktop (See Chapter 3).

Once you've dragged-and-dropped a file onto the printer icon, the program associated with the file is started and so is the printing – automatically!

Print Management

It is easy to find out which documents are currently printing and which are still waiting in the queue. Also shown is the document name, owner, size and when the print job was submitted.

You can pause, resume or cancel your print jobs submitted on a network printer attached to another PC. It isn't necessary to walk to the PC the printer is attached to.

You can also double-click the small printer icon displayed on the taskbar after a print job is submitted to display the print queue and status of your print jobs.

Epson
EPL-7500

Click on the printer icon your jobs are submitted to (Double-click if using Classic view).

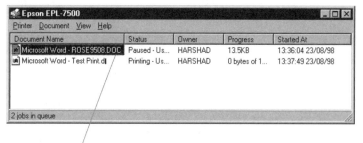

2 Click on the job you want to change the status of. Here Pause Printing from the Document menu was selected. This allows a job further down the queue to print before. Click on Pause Printing again to resume printing.

Note that whenever there is a problem (e.g. a paper jam), the small printer icon on the Taskbar displays a red warning circle with a question mark. Move your mouse over it for an

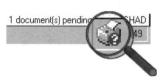

explanation, or double-click on it to display the print queue again (so that you can resume printing after correcting any problems.)

Configuration

You can configure many of your printer settings depending on the type of printer you have.

1 From the Printers folder, right-click once on the printer icon you want to configure.

2 In the shortcut menu, click on P<u>r</u>operties.

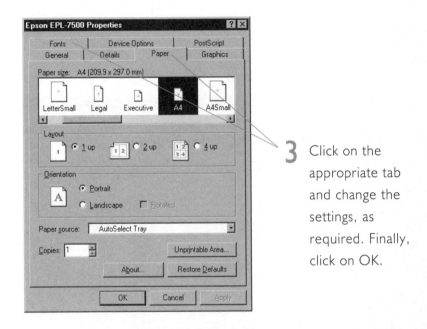

3 Click on the appropriate tab and change the settings, as required. Finally, click on OK.

Click on the Print <u>T</u>est Page button (from the General tab) after you have first installed your printer to ensure that it works as expected. If it doesn't, Windows will guide you through correcting the problem.

The Restore <u>D</u>efaults button is available from most tab settings so if you really make a mess of things, just click on this button.

Troubleshooting

Printing problems are common. If you experience difficulties, use the Windows Help system to resolve them.

1 Click on the Start button and then on Help.

2 Type "Printers" in the Help Index and display the "printers, troubleshooting" entry from the list.

3 Click here. Then follow the instructions given.

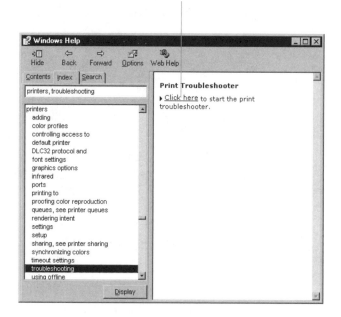

Networking

There is a built-in basic Networking capability within Windows 98. Networking allows you to share information and resources between several computers linked together.

Once set up, you will be able to easily share files and printers with your colleagues at work. It's also possible for all the computers in the network to access the company's Web site or pages (set up and stored on a local hard drive especially for this purpose) without ever connecting to, or dialling out to use, the Internet.

Covers

Chapter Nine

Network Basics

A network is a group of computers linked together so that you can work more efficiently.

One of the main advantages of using a network is that there is no need to transfer information between computers using floppy disks. Instead, the information can stay where it is and you simply allow other users to share it, or other users allow you to share their information. This sharing of information can be extended to sharing of devices, like the printer or modem.

Networking with Windows 98 in easy steps, in this same series of books, covers setting up the hardware and all other aspects in depth.

Since security may be an important consideration to you, it is possible to restrict access to information and resources by the use of passwords.

However, before you can use any of the networking features, you need to have the appropriate hardware installed. To network your computer to another, a special device, called *Network card* needs to be fitted. This controls the communication of your computer with another in the network (which also needs to have a network card). The computers are then physically connected, via the network cards, using special cables and connectors.

Identifying a Network Device

If any device (printer, disk drive, etc...) is a Network device rather than physically existing within your computer or directly attached to it, then the icon representing it within any of the views (e.g. My Computer, Windows Explorer) has a small cable at the base.

C on 'Comp3'
[F:]

This is a Network disk drive from another computer, comp3. You have access to its whole C hard disk drive through your logical drive F.

The Network Neighborhood

There is no 'u' in the American spelling of 'Neighborhood'.

If the Network is already set up on your computer the Network Neighborhood icon appears on the desktop. From here, you can access shared resources on other computers.

Network Neighborhood

1 Click on the Network Neighborhood icon.

Your own computer appears here too.

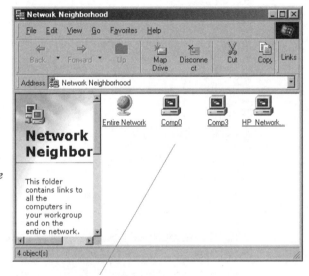

If you're currently using the Classic style (rather than Web style) view, double-click (rather than single-click) in steps 1-2.

2 If there are computers connected to your workgroup, they'll appear here. Also, by clicking on the Entire Network icon, computers not in your workgroup will appear. Click on any computer to see what you can access from it.

There is an entry in the left pane of Windows Explorer for the Network Neighborhood too – you can access the whole network from here also.

3 For example, from computer Comp0, you can access the whole of the C disk, two other folders, and a network printer connected to it.

Setting Up the Network Software

Before you can set up the software, the hardware must already be installed, as discussed.

If the Network Neighborhood icon appears on your desktop and Windows prompts you for a Network password when you switch on, the network is already set up on your computer. To install the software:

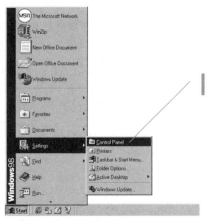

Click on the Start button, move over to Settings, and then click on Control Panel.

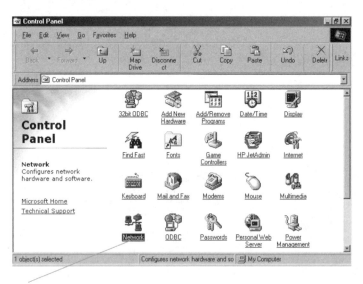

2 Select the Network icon.

Windows 98 auto-matically sets up other necessary network components when you install the Adapter.

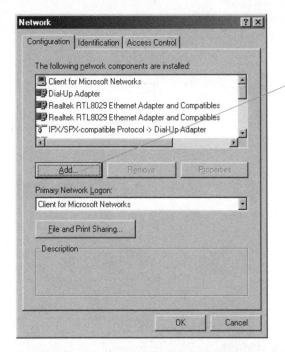

3 Click on Add... if your Adapter does not appear in the list displayed.

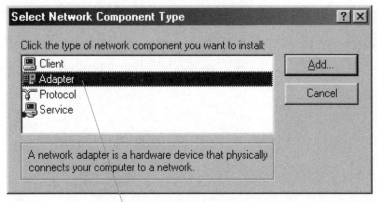

4 Click on Adapter to select it and then on the Add... button.

5 Follow the rest of the instructions, as given.

Naming your Computer on the Network

Once your Network software has been installed, you need to give your computer an identity on the network.

1 Still from within the Network box, click on the Identification tab at the top.

The decription helps other users link to your computer.

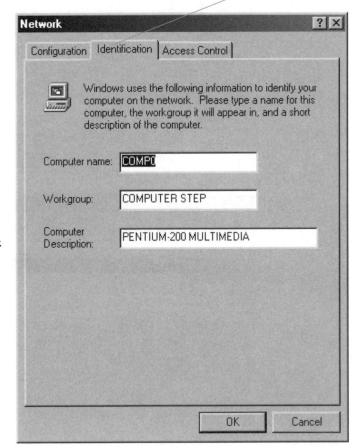

2 Type in your Computer name, Workgroup name, and a description of your computer. Then click OK.

Sharing your Folders or Printers

To be able to share your files/documents you need to share the folder they are in. You can also share the printers attached to your computer with other users networked to your computer. Before you start though, click on the <u>F</u>ile and Print Sharing... button in the Network dialog to ensure that file and printer sharing is set up.

To share a folder

To share an entire disk, right-click on a disk drive icon instead of a folder.

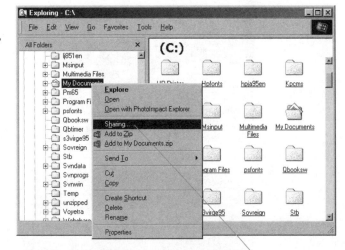

A little hand appears below the folder icon to indicate that it is shared:

My Documents

1   Right-click on the folder you want to share. Then click on the S<u>h</u>aring... option.

2   From the Sharing tab, click on the <u>S</u>hared As option.

3   Select <u>F</u>ull if you allow others to update your files and type password(s), if appropriate.

To share your printer

1 Click on the Start button, move pointer over Settings, and click on Printers.

2 Right-click on the printer you want to share, and then click on the Sharing... option.

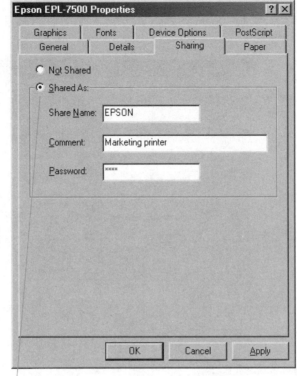

A little hand appears below the printer icon to indicate that it is shared:

Epson
EPL-7500

3 From the Sharing tab, click on the Shared As option. Then type a description to identify the printer and a password if you want to restrict access.

User-level access

So far we have looked at sharing of folders and printers by simply making them shareable and using a password perhaps to restrict access to certain people only. There is another way of giving permission to share your resources, called *user-level access control*. In order to set this up follow these steps:

Click on the Start button, move over to Settings, and then click on Control Panel.

If you're currently using the Classic style (rather than Web style) view, double-click (rather than single-click) in steps 2.

2 Click on the Network icon.

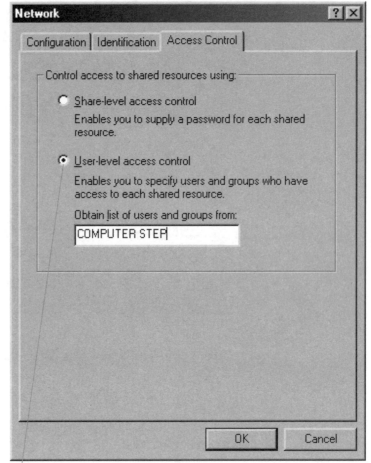

3 Click on the Access Control tab, and then on Userⁱlevel access control option.

4 Now, when you select the Sharing... option for folders or printers, a list of names is displayed and you can decide access rights for each one.

Using Shared Resources from other Computers

Once a folder or a disk from another networked computer is shared (see previous topic), you can access it from your Network Neighborhood icon (see earlier topic). Simply open the folder from the other computer to use the files it contains.

If you are frequently going to use the same shared folder, then it is best to assign a logical drive letter to it (e.g. E, F, G, ...). Then, you can access it from My Computer or Windows Explorer in exactly the same way as any of your own physical drives.

If the Map Drive icon doesn't appear in the Standard Buttons toolbar, select Start, Settings, Folder options..., View tab and ensure that 'Show Map Network Drive button in toolbar' is ticked.

Logical drives don't really exist – you are mapping, say, a folder on the hard disk C in another computer to a logical drive F on your computer. You cannot map it as the same letter C because you already use it for your own hard disk drive. You can use several letters to map different folders from one or more other computers you are connected to.

1 Click on the Map Drive icon in the Standard Buttons toolbar (see page 63) from any window (e.g. My Computer, Windows Explorer, Network Neighborhood).

Map
Drive

Click on Reconnect at logon option to ensure that this is automated when you log on (provided the computer in the path is on when you start yours).

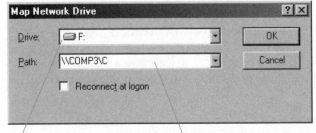

2 The next free drive letter appears here.

3 Type in the path for the folder (including the computer name).

...cont'd

 Create a shortcut to a network resource, like a drive or printer, you use frequently (see Chapter 3 – Creating a Shortcut).

You can click the arrow on the right to choose a different drive letter than the next available one, or choose a path used previously rather than typing it in.

Right-click on the My Computer icon or the Network Neighborhood icon to display a shortcut menu, from which you can select the option Map Network Drive... instead of selecting it from the toolbar icon inside the window.

Disconnecting from a Network Drive

You can also select Disconnect Network Drive... from the shortcut menu displayed by right-clicking on the My Computer or Network Neighborhood icons. Alternatively, click on the Disconnect icon next to the Map Drive icon in the Standard buttons toolbar. Either way, you'll see:

 To not see this dialog, simply right-click on a connected drive icon from any window and select Disconnect from the shortcut menu.

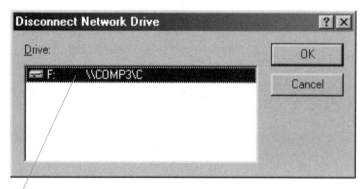

Click on the path you want to disconnect and then on OK.

Network Printer

 Print a Test page before printing too many pages to ensure that the printer works as expected.

Before you can use a shared printer set up on another computer on the network, you will need to set it up again on your computer as a Network printer (See Chapter 8 on Printing). Then print your documents as normal using the new network printer.

Customising

This chapter shows you how to change the way Windows 98 looks on your computer and how to alter other settings to suit your requirements. Additionally, you'll learn to set up Windows 98 for multiple users. Finally, there is also advice for users with special needs.

Covers

Chapter Ten

Colours

You can use up to 9 monitors with Windows 98, at any one time. This allows you to:

- *work with one large, overall desktop (great for certain types of games)*
- *run different programs on each monitor*
- *copy items between monitors*
- *test your own web graphics at different monitor resolutions, to view them as others will.*

First, switch your PC off. Install the relevant graphics adapters. Switch your machine back on and follow the on-screen setup procedure.

To change monitor settings, refer to the Settings tab of the Display Properties dialog (route: activate the Display icon in Control Panel).

You can change most of the colours you see in Windows and Windows applications to suit your taste. You can't however change the colours of the icons.

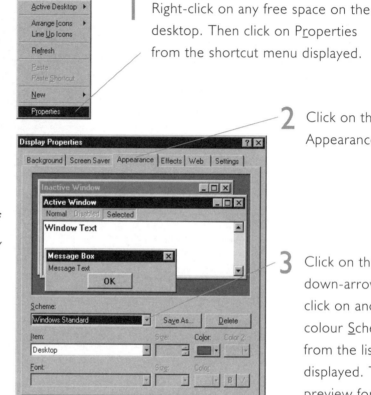

1 Right-click on any free space on the desktop. Then click on Properties from the shortcut menu displayed.

2 Click on the Appearance tab.

3 Click on this down-arrow then click on another colour Scheme from the list displayed. The preview for it is displayed on top.

4 Click on OK to confirm changes and close this window, or on Apply just to confirm the changes made.

You can change the colour of individual items instead of the whole scheme. Just click on the item from the preview (e.g. Active Window title bar). Then alter the Size/Color by using the arrows next to these. Use Color 2 to create a 'fading into' effect from the first colour. If the item chosen includes text, you can change its font, size and colour too.

Patterns and Wallpapers

Microsoft also sells an add-on – 98 Plus – which supplies (among other things) additional wallpapers and backgrounds, organised as themes.

You can change the desktop background with a pattern or a wallpaper of your choice. If you use a pattern and then a wallpaper, only the wallpaper will be displayed.

| 1 | Right-click on any free space on the desktop. Then click on Properties from the shortcut menu displayed. |

To select a background pattern instead of a wallpaper, first ensure None is chosen as the Wallpaper. Click on Pattern... Select a pattern in the Pattern dialog, then click on OK.
Finally, follow step 4.

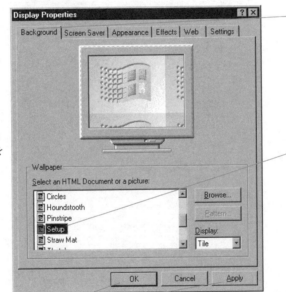

2 Click on the Background tab.

3 Click on a wallpaper you like.

Display options: Center displays a wallpaper once in the centre, Tile and Stretch fill the whole desktop – either by repeating the basic design or stretching it.

4 Click on OK to confirm changes and close this window, or on Apply just to confirm the changes made.

As an alternative to step 3, click on the Browse... button to locate and use a HTML (Web) page as a wallpaper. Note, however, that HTML files cannot be centred or tiled.

Screen Savers

Screen savers are images displayed on the screen when there is no activity for some time. This is supposed to prevent your screen from burn-out.

Right-click on any free space on the desktop. Then click on Properties from the shortcut menu displayed.

2 Click on the Screen Saver tab.

This Settings button allows you to set Power Management properties – ensure Turn off monitor is set to: Never. Otherwise the Screen saver may never start but instead your monitor switches off temporarily.

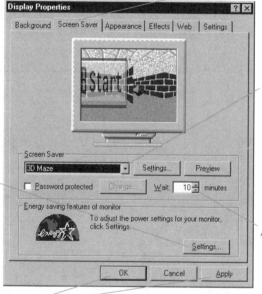

3 Click on the pull-down arrow and select a Screen saver.

4 Click on up/down arrows to change the time of inactivity before the screen saver starts.

This Settings... button next to the Screen Saver allows you to vary the default variables of a screen saver (e.g. colours, speed, size) and depends on the screen saver.

5 Click on OK to confirm changes and close this window, or on Apply just to confirm the changes made.

Click on the Preview button to see the screen saver in action. To continue working after a screen saver display, press any key or move your mouse a little.

Multiple Users

See page 24 for how to log off so another user can use your PC.

Windows 98 has a special wizard you can run – the Enable Multi-user Settings wizard – which sets up your computer for use by more than one user. This involves:

A. setting up unique user names and passwords for each user

B. creating multiple desktop profiles (customised desktops, including Programs, Start menu, Favorites, and My Documents). Each user has his/her own profile.

Rerun the wizard as many times as there are users.

1 Click on the Users icon from the Control Panel window (Start menu, Settings).

2 Follow the instructions given in a series of dialog boxes.

At the end of the process, Windows restarts. When prompted, log on by typing in the user name and password you set up in the wizard. Then customise your profile – changes you make are automatically saved in your name.

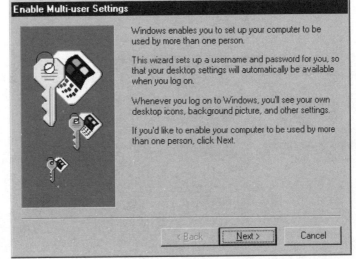

Enable Multi-user Settings

Windows enables you to set up your computer to be used by more than one person.

This wizard sets up a username and password for you, so that your desktop settings will automatically be available when you log on.

Whenever you log on to Windows, you'll see your own desktop icons, background picture, and other settings.

If you'd like to enable your computer to be used by more than one person, click Next.

< Back | Next > | Cancel

In order to create separate user profiles, you must grant permission from Control panel, Passwords, User Profiles tab.

3 Click on the Back button to change options from the previous box, or Cancel to abandon the procedure altogether. Otherwise, continue to select Next until the last box which replaces this button with Finish.

Date and Time

Your computer has an internal clock which can be reset at any time. It can be displayed on the Taskbar at all times so that you always know what time it is while you are working.

Date and time data are used by other programs and Windows itself.

To display the clock

Click on the Start button, move your mouse pointer over Settings, and click on the Taskbar & Start Menu... option.

You can also right-click on any blank section of the Taskbar and click on Properties from the shortcut menu to produce this same window.

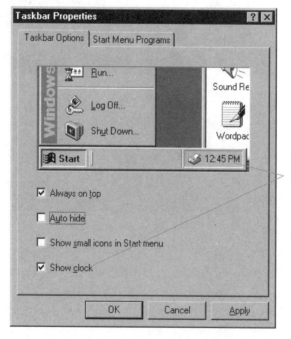

2 Click on the Show clock option so that it's ticked and displayed on the Taskbar preview. Then click on OK.

To display the date

Move your mouse pointer over the time displayed on the Taskbar and leave it there for a few seconds. The current date then pops up.

To reset date/time

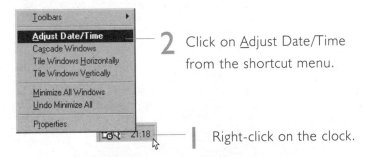

2 Click on Adjust Date/Time from the shortcut menu.

1 Right-click on the clock.

Click on the Time Zone tab to change the Greenwich Mean Time for another country.

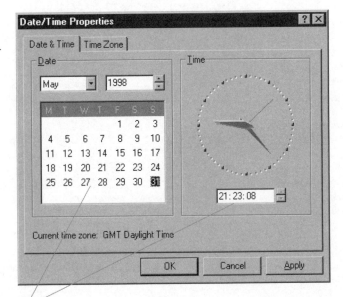

3 Click on another day (or change the month/year first above), or click inside the time box and either use the arrows or type the new time in the box. Finally, click on OK.

Mouse

If you're currently using the Classic style (rather than Web style) view, double-click (rather than single-click) in step 1.

The make of mouse attached to your computer may be different from the Microsoft mouse shown here. However, similar customising options will still be offered.

Mouse

Click on the Mouse icon from the Control Panel window (Start menu, Settings).

Click on other tabs to change other settings for your mouse.

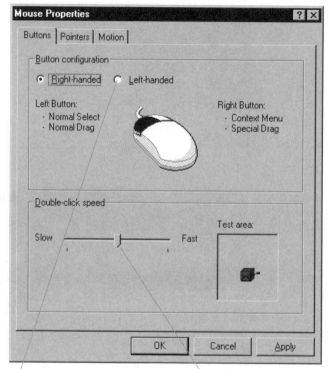

If your PC has a USB (Universal Serial Bus) port, you can add new serial devices (e.g. mice, keyboards and modems) without having to install an adapter card, and without first switching off your machine. Windows 98 automatically detects the new device and installs the necessary driver (software which runs it).

2 If you're left-handed, click on the Left-handed option.

3 Drag this slider to increase or decrease the speed at which a double-click is recognised. Then test the speed by double-clicking on the object in the Test area. Finally, click on OK.

Keyboard

Like your mouse, your keyboard settings can be changed to suit your personal preference.

If you're currently using the Classic style (rather than Web style) view, double-click (rather than single-click) in step 1.

Keyboard

Click on the Keyboard icon from the Control Panel window (Start menu, Settings).

Click on other tabs to change other settings for your keyboard.

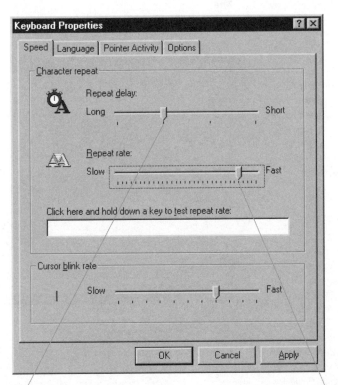

2 Drag the Repeat delay slider to set the time your computer waits before it starts repeating the first key when you have held it down.

3 Drag the Repeat rate slider to set how fast or slow a key repeats itself when you hold it down. Click in the test box and hold down a key to test the repeat rate. Finally, click on OK.

Multimedia

If you're currently using the Classic style (rather than Web style) view, double-click (rather than single-click) in step 1.

Multimedia, as the name suggests, is the integration of several media formats including video and audio. All new computers nowadays have a CD-ROM drive fitted and many also have a sound card and speakers.

Multimedia

| Click on the Multimedia icon from the Control Panel window (Start menu, Settings).

Use the multimedia programs available with Windows 98, like CD Player and Media Player, to play audio CDs and view animations.

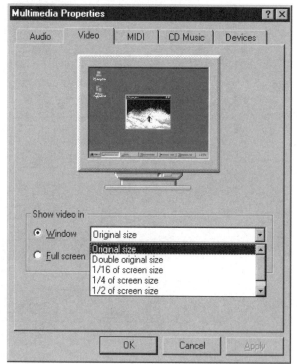

Windows 98 supports high-density DVD drives (an advanced CD technology). DVD drives hold much more information than normal CD-ROM drives; you can therefore use them to play full-length films (as well as – generally – normal CDs).

2 Click on the relevant tabs and change settings as required. Then click on OK.

Sounds

If you're currently using the Classic style (rather than Web style) view, double-click (rather than single-click) in step 1.

You can assign different sounds to events that occur when using Windows, like when starting Windows, when you exit Windows, and so on. These will only work, of course, if you have a sound card fitted.

Sounds

| Click on the Sounds icon from the Control Panel window (Start menu, Settings).

Windows 98 lets you watch TV on your PC, providing you've installed the necessary TV tuner card.

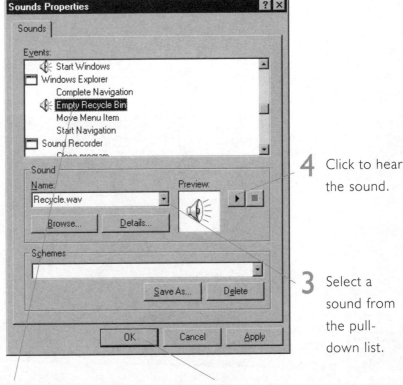

4 Click to hear the sound.

3 Select a sound from the pull-down list.

You can also access live video/audio material across the Internet (or a local intranet) with minimal impact on system performance.

To do this, however, you must have installed Microsoft NetShow Player 2.0 (located within the Multimedia section of Windows Setup).

2 Click on the event you want to add/change the sound for.

5 Click to link the sound to the event.

Taskbar

The principal components of the Taskbar, usually at the bottom of the screen, are:

- the Start button.

- the clock and printer status icons.

- task buttons for each open application.

- the Quick Launch toolbar.

To move/resize the Taskbar

1 Drag the Taskbar (from a clear area) to the top, bottom, left or right screen edges.

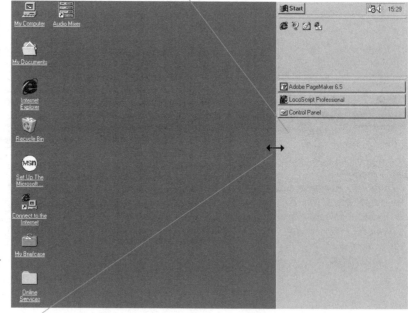

2 Move your mouse pointer over the inside edge of the Taskbar so that it changes to a double-headed arrow. Then drag it in either direction to change the width of the Taskbar.

To change Taskbar properties

Right-click on any free space on the Taskbar and then click on Properties from the shortcut menu displayed. (Or click on the Start menu, move the mouse over Settings and click on Taskbar & Start Menu...).

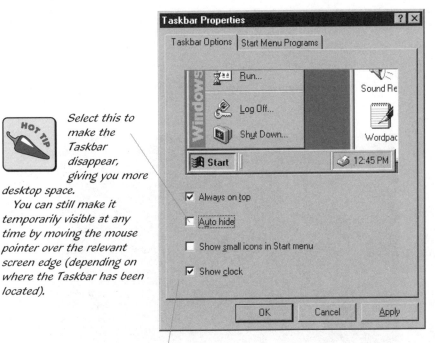

Select this to make the Taskbar disappear, giving you more desktop space.

You can still make it temporarily visible at any time by moving the mouse pointer over the relevant screen edge (depending on where the Taskbar has been located).

Click on the options required (so that they are ticked) or click on ticked options to turn off the feature. Then click on OK.

Accessibility Features

To launch the Magnifier directly, click on Start, Programs, Accessories, Accessibility, Magnifier. Complete the Magnifier dialog. Click on OK.

To close the Magnifier, right-click its button in the Taskbar. Click on Close in the shortcut menu.

With Windows 98, Microsoft recognises that some users are likely to have difficulty with certain operating tasks. As a result, you can opt to make use of specific workarounds. For example, if you have trouble using a mouse (perhaps because of Repetitive Strain Injury), you can opt to use the Numeric Keypad on the right of your keyboard to mimic mouse operation. Or, if you're visually impaired, you can use a special Windows feature known as the Microsoft Magnifier to provide an enlargement of the screen area currently under the mouse pointer:

As you move the mouse in the main body of the screen, an enlarged view is shown in the Magnifier above

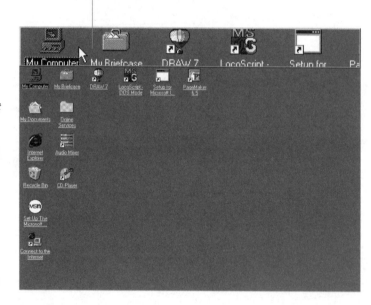

To implement the relevant Accessibility features, click on Start, Programs, Accessories, Accessibility, Accessibility Wizard.

Complete the dialogs which launch, clicking on Next to move on to successive screens. Finally, click on Finish to complete the wizard.

Caveat

The Magnifier is only intended to provide a very basic level of support for the visually impaired. Visit the following special Microsoft Web site:

http://www.microsoft.com/enable

for information about more effective programs.

Accessories

Accessories are basic programs and utilities provided free with Windows 98. If a program described here is not available on your computer, install the relevant Windows 98 component.

Covers

Chapter Eleven

WordPad

Wordpad.exe

WordPad is a basic word processor used to create and edit documents.

| Click on Start and move the mouse over Programs, then Accessories, and then click on WordPad.

HOT TIP

To edit text in WordPad, do the following, as appropriate:

- *Move the mouse pointer to the start of the text you want to edit – it will change to an I-beam. Then click on the mouse and drag it to the end of the text-string you want to edit. The selected piece of text will be highlighted.*

- *Press the Del key on your keyboard to delete the selected text, or type in some new text to replace it.*

- *Drag the selected text to another part of the text block to move it, or press the Control key when dragging to make a copy of it elsewhere.*

Open a document

Helps you find a document

Click to insert today's date (or time) in a specific format

Undo

Align text

Print and Print Preview

Change colour

Save a document

Click to create bullets automatically

Creating a new document

| To create a new document, simply start typing in WordPad

or

Click on New... from the File menu. This will allow you to choose the type of document to create (e.g. Word) although you can specify this when you save the document. Click OK.

Paint

Mspaint.exe

Paint is a basic drawing and painting program. It can also be used to enhance images scanned using a scanner.

You can use a better accessory – Kodak Imaging – to edit scanned images (see page 157).

Click on Start and move the mouse over Programs, then Accessories, and then click on Paint.

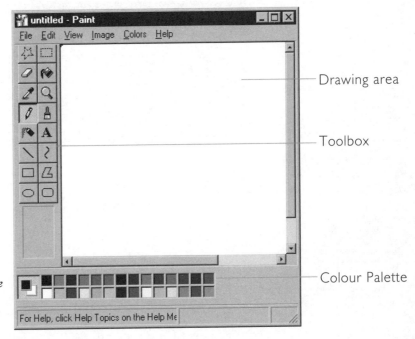

Drawing area

Toolbox

Colour Palette

To draw in Paint, select a tool (e.g. Brush). Then drag the mouse in the Drawing area. (If you make a mistake, press Ctrl+Shift+N – then start all over again.)

Toolbox

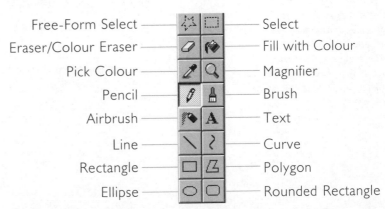

Free-Form Select —— Select
Eraser/Colour Eraser —— Fill with Colour
Pick Colour —— Magnifier
Pencil —— Brush
Airbrush —— Text
Line —— Curve
Rectangle —— Polygon
Ellipse —— Rounded Rectangle

To zoom in on part of a drawing, click on the Magnifier tool. Then click the relevant section.

Character Map

Charmap.exe

The Character Map enables you to use characters and special symbols from other character sets in your document.

I Click on Start and move the mouse over Programs, Accessories, System Tools. Then click on Character Map.

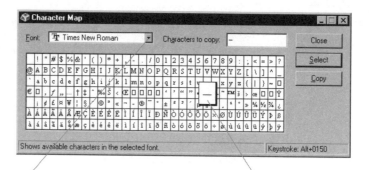

Step 4 – You can use a different method. Look at the keystroke combination in the bottom right of the dialog:

To use this, go to the relevant document. Press the Num Lock key. Hold down Alt, and type out the numerical component (in this case, 0150) on the Numerical keypad at the right of your keyboard. Release Alt, then press Num Lock again.

2 Click and select the font from the drop-down list.

3 Click and hold down the mouse to magnify the character.

4 Double-click on a character to send it to the 'Characters to copy' box (or click on a character once and press the Select button). Repeat this for as many characters as you want to include. Then click on the Copy button to copy the character(s) in the 'Characters to copy' box to the Clipboard. From here you can paste the character(s) into your document in the normal way.

See the next topic for how to use the Clipboard.

Clipboard Viewer

Clipbrd.exe

The Clipboard is a temporary storage area. It is used to transfer information (text and graphics) between applications and within the same document.

Whenever you select an object/text from an application and click on Cut or Copy from the Edit menu, it goes into the Clipboard. The Print Screen button on your keyboard also copies the whole screen to the Clipboard, while Alt+Print Screen copies just the active window. To insert the contents of the Clipboard somewhere else later on, click on Paste from the Edit menu. (See Cut, Copy and Paste in Chapter 3, Working with Programs.)

It is not necessary to use Clipboard Viewer to perform the Cut, Copy and Paste functions. However, you must remember that the contents of the Clipboard are overwritten if you copy something else into it, and cleared when you quit Windows. Therefore the main benefit of using the Clipboard Viewer is to save its contents for subsequent retrieval.

1 Click on Start and move the mouse over Programs, Accessories, System Tools. Then click on Clipboard Viewer.

Press the Del key to clear the contents of the clipboard. In the Clear Clipboard message, click on Yes.

A clip art image, copied to the Clipboard

2 Click on File, Save As... to save the current contents of the clipboard as a .clp file.

Media Player

Mplayer.exe

The Media Player lets you play/view video, sound and pictures – a variety of these are stored on the Windows 98 CD-ROM disc.

The example on this page shows Media Player running an ActiveMovie clip.

I Click on Start and move the mouse pointer over Programs, then Accessories, Entertainment. Finally, click on Media Player.

2 Click on Open in the File menu. Select a multimedia file.

To stop a clip before it's reached the end, see below.

You can also use Media Player to play audio CDs. Click on CD Audio in the Device menu. Insert the CD into your drive and click on:

3 Click here to begin playing the clip.

Media Player buttons

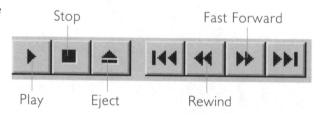

Stop   Fast Forward

Play   Eject   Rewind

Kodak Imaging

Kodakimg.exe

Kodak Imaging is a more advanced method of enhancing scanned images. You can also:

- work with a wider range of graphics file formats (including faxes)

- annotate images

1 Click on Start. Move the mouse pointer over Programs, then Accessories. Click on Imaging.

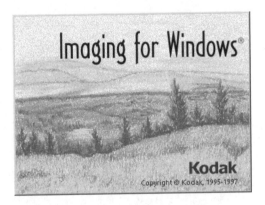

2 Click on Open in the File menu and select a graphics file. Alternatively, click on New in the File menu.

3 To edit the file, use the Annotation toolbar in the bottom lefthand corner of the screen:

To customise how any of the tools work (apart from the Selector), right-click any button. Complete the dialog which launches, then click OK.

Freehand Line Straight Line Filled Rectangle Note tool Rubber Stamp

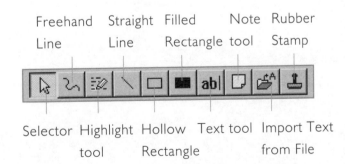

Selector Highlight tool Hollow Rectangle Text tool Import Text from File

Phone Dialer

Dialer.exe

This is a useful program, especially if you don't have a speed dial facility on your phone. Before you can use it though, you'll need a modem connected to your computer and it must be the type you can connect your phone into.

I Click on Start and move the mouse over <u>P</u>rograms, then Accessories, Communications. Then click on Phone Dialer.

Click on the drop-down list to access previously dialled

numbers.

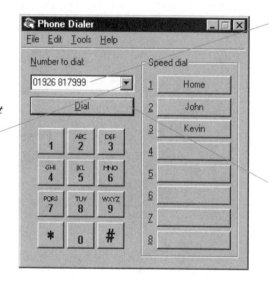

2 Type in the phone number or click on buttons simulating buttons on a phone.

3 Click on <u>D</u>ial.

4 Wait for the number to be dialled. When you hear a high pitched tone, follow the on-screen instructions.

5 Use your telephone as normal.

Speed dialling

To change or delete a Speed dial number, click on the Edit menu in the Phone Dialer dialog (see earlier). Then click on Speed Dial...

| Click on one of the empty Speed dial buttons to program it.

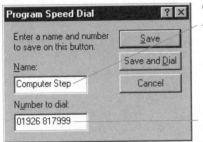

2 Type a name associated with the number you want to see on the Speed dial button.

3 Type the telephone number.

Standard settings

You can also access the Dialing Properties dialog by activating this icon:

Telephony

in Control Panel.

| Click on Tools and then Dialing Properties...

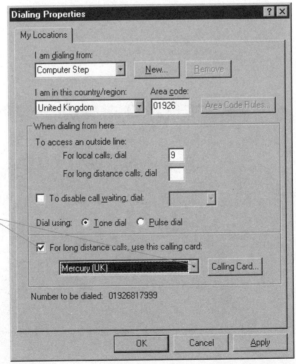

2 Complete this dialog. Then click on OK.

Click here if you use a calling card. Click on the arrow, then select the card in the list. Now the card will always be used when you make a call.

Calculator

Calc.exe

The Calculator provides both Standard and Scientific calculators.

1 Click on Start and move the mouse over Programs, then Accessories. Finally, click on Calculator.

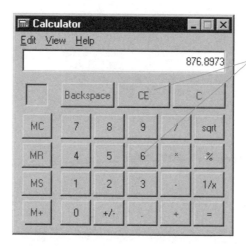

2 Click on the relevant buttons (similar to buttons on a hand-held calculator) or type the values from the keyboard.

3 To perform trigonometric and statistical functions, click on the View menu and then Scientific.

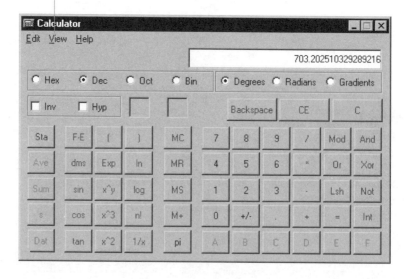

System Tools

Windows 98 includes a set of tools to enhance the performance and reliability of your entire computer system. Use this chapter to ensure you continue to work efficiently and securely.

Covers

Chapter Twelve

Disk Properties

As for other objects in Windows 98, you can easily access the Properties dialog box for a disk. Then, you can check general details about your disk, like the amount of free space available, and perform *housekeeping* routines like Defragment the disk, Backup, etc.

To format a floppy disk, right-click its icon in My Computer or Windows Explorer. Click on Format... in the shortcut menu. In the Format dialog, select Quick (to perform a rapid format if the disk has already been formatted) or Full. Click on Start.

When the format is complete, click on Close twice.

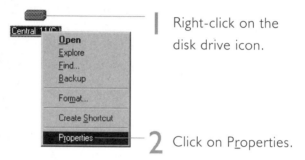

1 Right-click on the disk drive icon.

2 Click on Properties.

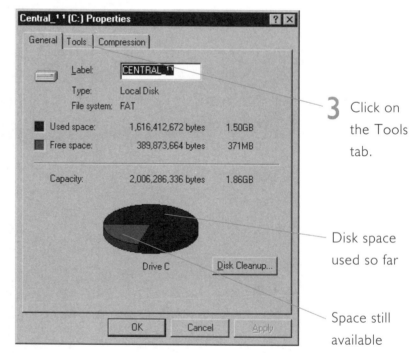

3 Click on the Tools tab.

Disk space used so far

Space still available

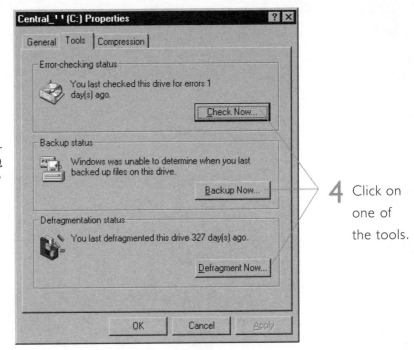

You can schedule ScanDisk, the Defragmenter and Backup (or any other Windows program). (See page 180 for how to do this).

4 Click on one of the tools.

For another way to schedule disk maintenance activities, see the Maintenance Wizard topic on pages 170–171.

Check Now...	looks for disk errors and fixes them. See ScanDisk (later in this chapter).
Backup Now...	allows you to make secure copies of your data. See Backup (later in this chapter).
Defragment Now...	reorganises the disk to speed up file access. See Disk Defragmenter (later in this chapter).

ScanDisk

ScanDisk allows you to analyse and repair problems with your disk. Although it is common to use it on your hard disk (even though it may be compressed using DriveSpace 3 – see later), you can use it on removable disks too.

Click on ScanDisk from Start button, Programs, Accessories, System Tools or run it from Disk Properties.

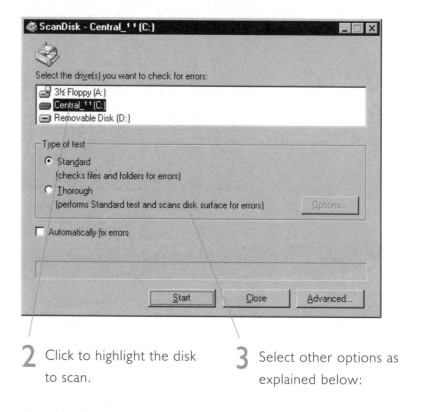

2 Click to highlight the disk to scan.

3 Select other options as explained below:

The Standard test will perform basic checks like looking for *Lost file fragments* – over time files can become fragmented on a disk (see Disk Defragmenter for more details), and so different parts are linked together by pointers. If these pointers are corrupted, then some parts of a file cannot be retrieved. ScanDisk can find these fragments and either delete them from the disk to free up space or create special files to write them into. You can try and recover the fragments lost from these files, but more often than not you will not be successful.

Another standard check is for *cross-linked files*. This is when there are two pointers addressing the same file block. Pointers have to be unique so this condition is an error. It is worth opting to Make copies of the file block that has two pointers in the hope that at least one of the files can be rescued. Select this and other options from the Advanced... button and the subsequent dialog box.

The default options shown are recommended.

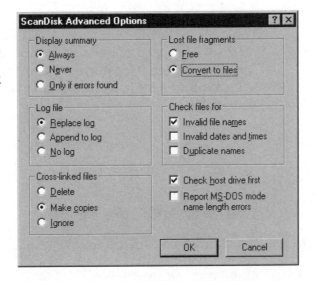

Although a Thorough scan takes longer, it is worth running it frequently on your important disk.

The Thorough scan option performs a disk surface scan too. This reads and writes back each *cluster* (or allocation unit) on disk to ensure that there are no problems. If the disk had been compressed by DriveSpace (see later), it will also check that data can be decompressed from it.

The surface scan can fix errors by trying to write data from *bad sectors* found on disk to another area on the disk.

Disk Defragmenter

A file is not always stored in a single contiguous disk location. It may be split and stored in different areas of the disk, particularly if you are frequently updating and deleting your files. This fragmentation doesn't damage the files, but when you want to access them, it takes longer. This is because first of all, at the end of each file fragment, a pointer needs to be read to give the address of where the next fragment is stored on disk. Then, the disk heads may need to move to an entirely different part of the disk to retrieve the chained fragment. This process can continue depending on how fragmented a particular file has become, making the access inefficient and slow.

You can reorganise your disk so that each file stored (perhaps as several pieces scattered all over the disk) is read and then written back in continuous storage locations. This will speed up access to all your files when you need to use them again.

Click on Disk Defragmenter from Start button, Programs, Accessories, System Tools. Or run it from Disk Properties.

2 Select the drive. Then click on OK.

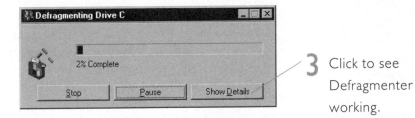

3 Click to see Defragmenter working.

Your main hard disk drive will take at least half an hour to defragment, depending on:

- how fragmented it is
- its size
- the speed of your computer

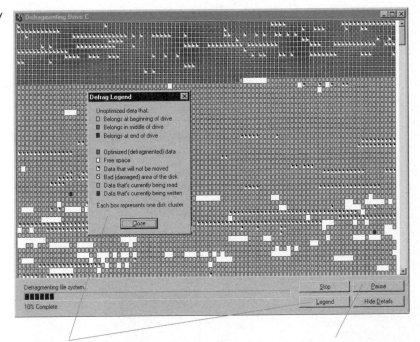

Click on the Legend button to see what the different coloured squares are.

Click to temporarily pause the defragmenting. This will speed up other Windows 98 programs you may be running at the same time.

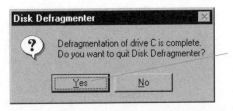

4 Click here.

DriveSpace 3

DriveSpace 3 prepares your disk drive so that all the files you store are compressed. This effectively has the effect of roughly doubling your disk capacity. Although it is common to install DriveSpace 3 on your hard disk, you can also install it on floppy disks, especially if you're using them for backups.

| Click on DriveSpace from Start button, Programs, Accessories, System Tools.

Compressing your main C drive can take a long time so schedule this task at the end of a day or a quiet period.

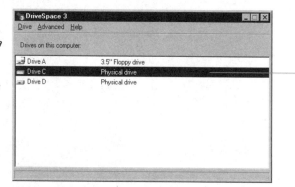

2 Select the drive to compress.

Drives which have had the FAT 32 file storage system imposed (see later) cannot be compressed.

3 Click on the Drive menu, and then Compress...

...cont'd

Although rare, some files may become corrupted when DriveSpace 3 is running. It is therefore advisable to back up your data before beginning the compression process.

DriveSpace 3 can only directly compress hard disks which are up to 1 Gb in size. However, if your hard disk is larger than this, it can create a second drive for all the uncompressed space. It needs to create this new second host drive anyway to move some system files into because they cannot be compressed.

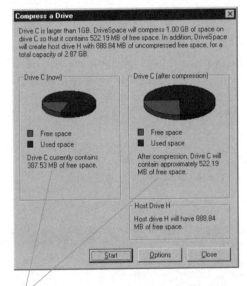

If you run into any problems with DriveSpace 3, run the Troubleshooter.

Click on the Start button, then Help. Ensure the Index tab is selected. Type in 'DriveSpace 3' and press Enter. In the Topics Found dialog, double-click 'DriveSpace 3 Troubleshooter'. In the Topic window, click:

Click here

Follow the on-screen instructions.

4 Compare the benefit of compressing your drive and click on Start if you are going to gain substantial Free space.

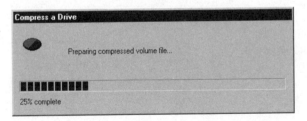

5 When compression is complete, click on Close in the Compress a Drive dialog above.

Maintenance Wizard

You can use a special wizard – the Maintenance Wizard – to:

- make your programs run faster (by running the Disk Defragmenter)

- troubleshoot your hard disk (by running ScanDisk)

- make more space available on your hard disk (by deleting unnecessary files e.g. temporary Internet and Windows files)

See the tips in the Disk Properties topic earlier for other ways to schedule activities.

The Maintenance Wizard works by scheduling: you specify when it runs, and the operations it carries out. You can, however, also have Windows 98 carry out the specified tasks at any time – see the DON'T FORGET tip on the left.

When you run the wizard for the first time, this dialog does not launch. Instead, simply complete the dialogs which appear.

| Click on Maintenance Wizard from Start button, Programs, Accessories, System Tools.

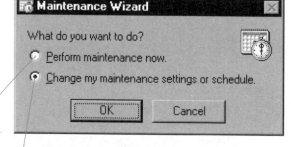

Click here: then click on OK (omit steps 2–5) to have Windows perform preset maintenance tasks now.

2 Click here. Then click on OK.

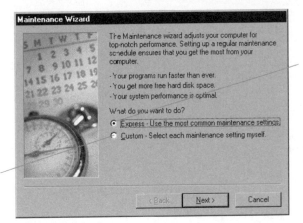

3 Click here.
Then click on
<u>N</u>ext.

*Click on here:
(and complete
the dialogs
which launch)
for more
control over maintenance
tasks. For instance, you can
specify which programs run
automatically when
Windows 98 starts, thereby
reducing load time.*

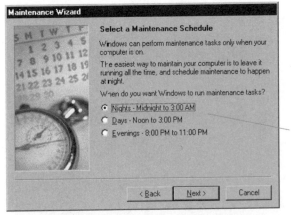

4 Select a
scheduling
period. Then
click on <u>N</u>ext.

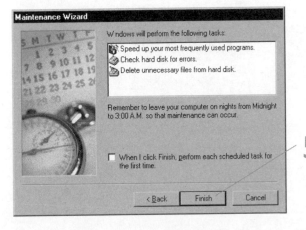

5 Click on
Finish.

Disk Cleanup

Use the Disk Cleanup utility to remove the following kinds of transient Windows files:

- Temporary files

- Deleted files in the Recycle Bin

- Downloaded Internet programs

Click on Start, Programs, Accessories, System Tools. Then click on Disk Cleanup.

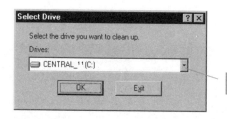

Click the arrow, then select a drive. Click on OK.

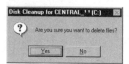

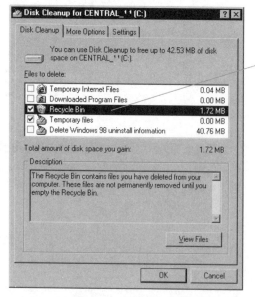

2 Select one or more categories (a ✔ appears in the box). Then click on OK.

Windows Update

To use Windows Update, you must have a live Internet connection.

You can use Windows Update to download the latest drivers and system updates/enhancements, thus ensuring that your PC's Windows installation is always up-to-date.

Windows Update automatically accesses a centralised, World Wide Web site.

| Click on Windows Update... from Start button, Settings.

Windows Update also provides product assistance information.

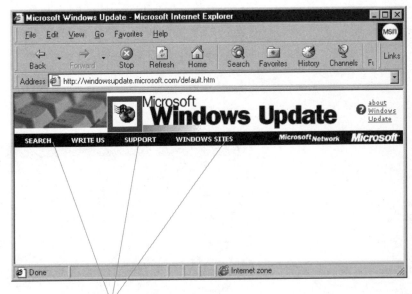

You can use the Update Wizard Uninstall to reinstate drivers for which you've installed updated versions.

Click on Start, Programs, Accessories, System Tools, System Information. Click on Update Wizard Uninstall in the Tools menu. Follow the on-screen instructions.

2 Click on the relevant links and follow the on-screen instructions.

System File Checker

System File Checker is a utility which:

- verifies your system files

- automatically reinstates any files which are corrupted

1 Click on Start, Programs, Accessories, System Tools, System Information. Click on System File Checker in the Tools menu.

2 In the System File Checker dialog, ensure Scan for altered files is selected. Then click on Start. System File Checker scans your system for altered/corrupted/deleted files.

3 Complete this dialog. Select Restore file to have Windows replace the flagged file.

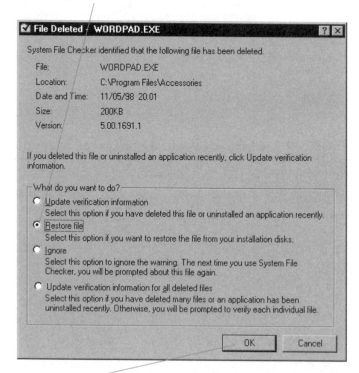

4 Click on OK.

5 Ensure the location of the correct file is shown here.

Repeat steps 3-6 for as many files as need to be restored.

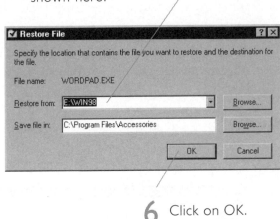

6 Click on OK.

System File Checker restores the file, and continues searching.

When the search is complete:

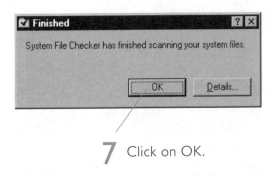

7 Click on OK.

8 Click on Close in the System File Checker dialog.

System Information

Using the System Information utility, you can gather detailed configuration information into one convenient file. This provides a lot of technical data about the way your system is set up.

In the illustration below, the System Information utility is supplying basic information about the display adapter fitted.

> Click on Start, Programs, Accessories, System Tools. Then click on System Information.

Data is often organised under three headings:

- *Brief Information*
- *Advanced Information*
- *History (details of changes)*

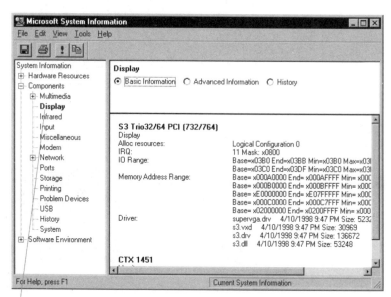

System Information provides access to other useful tools e.g:

- *Registry Checker – automatically (and manually) backs up your system settings.*

- *System Configuration Utility – an advanced tool which helps you fine-tune your system.*

2 Click on a topic to display the relevant details.

The Windows Report Tool

You can use a special tool within System Information to create a file which can be emailed to your technical support contact. This file contains all relevant system settings/configuration of your computer to help the technician.

When you've finished using System Information, press Alt+F4 to close it.

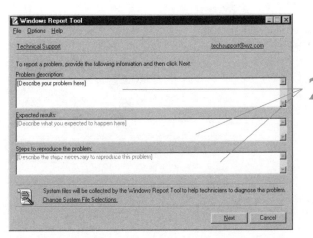

By default, Windows Report Tool files are saved (with the extension .CAB) in the following folder:

\Windows\Helpdesk\Winrep

Click on Windows Report Tool in the Tools menu.

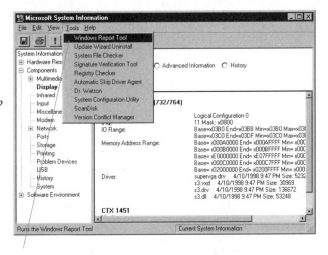

The Windows Report Tool includes your system files in the CAB file it produces.

2 Complete these fields, then click on Next.

3 Follow the further on-screen instructions.

Power Management

If you have a modern PC (with Advanced Power Management), you can save power by having Windows 98:

If your computer uses ACPI (Advanced Configuration and Power Interface), you can also:

- *put it on standby (especially useful for portable computers)*

- *hibernate it (more advanced – everything in memory is saved to disk).*

1. turn off your monitor

2. turn off your hard disk

You can specify the intervals at which these shutoffs occur. You can also save these setting combinations as 'power schemes', which makes applying them even easier.

Power Management settings

| Click on Start, Settings, Control Panel.

If you're currently using the Classic style (rather than Web style) view, double-click (rather than single-click) in step 2.

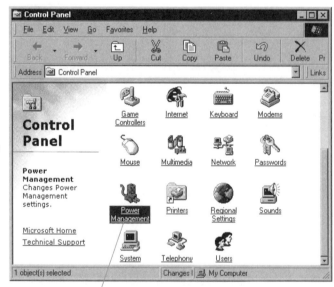

2 Click on Power Management.

3 Now perform steps 4 and 7 if you want to apply a preset power scheme OR steps 5–7 to apply individual settings.

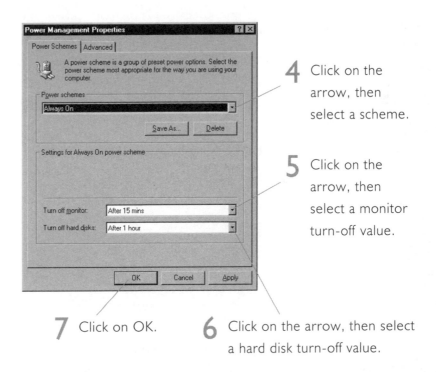

4 Click on the arrow, then select a scheme.

5 Click on the arrow, then select a monitor turn-off value.

7 Click on OK.

6 Click on the arrow, then select a hard disk turn-off value.

Creating a power scheme

1 Follow the previous steps 1–2 and 5–6.

2 Click on this button: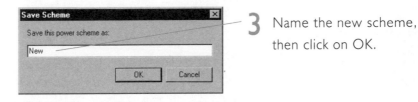

3 Name the new scheme, then click on OK.

4 Follow step 7.

Scheduling

You can have any Windows program run automatically at the time and interval you specify.

| Click on the Scheduled Tasks icon in My Computer. Alternatively, choose it from Start, Programs, Accessories, System Tools, Scheduled Tasks.

If you're currently using the Classic style (rather than Web style) view, double-click (rather than single-click) in steps 1-2.

2 Click on the Add Scheduled Task icon.

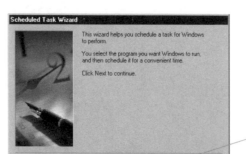

3 Click on Next.

Windows uses a special wizard – the Scheduled Task Wizard – to automate scheduling.

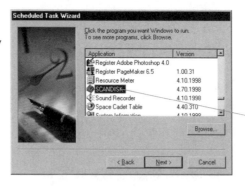

4 Click on a program entry. Then click on Next.

5 Click on the Back button to change options from the previous box, or Cancel to abandon the procedure altogether. Otherwise, continue to complete the dialogs, selecting Next until the Finish box appears. Click on this to implement your scheduling.

FAT 32 Drive Converter

There are several caveats to using FAT 32:

You can use the FAT 32 utility to convert your hard disk drive from the standard FAT (File Allocation Table) method of storing data to the newer FAT 32 system. The results of doing this are likely to be:

- considerably more free hard disk space (up to several hundred megabytes)

- programs start faster

- there are fewer drains on your PC's system resources

- *your hard drive must be over 512 megabytes*
- *you can't use DriveSpace 3 on converted drives*
- *if you convert your drive, you lose the ability to uninstall Windows 98 and revert to your previous installation*
- *you can't revert to the original FAT system*
- *if you have antivirus software on your PC, it may not recognise FAT 32 – check with your supplier*

Click on Start, Programs, Accessories, System Tools. Then click on Drive Converter (FAT 32).

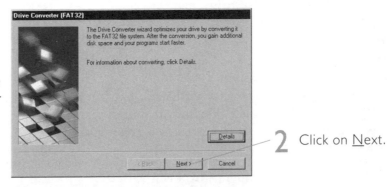

2 Click on Next.

Consider allowing the Converter to backup your files before conversion.

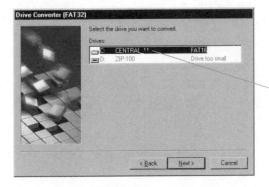

3 Click on a drive. Then click on Next.

4 Follow the on-screen instructions. (In particular, see the DON'T FORGET tip.)

Backup and Restore

You can restore backed up data onto your hard disk.

Click on Start, Programs, Accessories, System Tools, Backup. Select Restore backed up files, then click on OK. In the dialogs which appear, specify:

- *the backup file*

- *the backup job*

- *the file(s) you want restored*

- *where you want the file(s) restored to*

- *whether Restore should overwrite existing files with the same name*

When the Start button appears, click on it to begin the restore operation.

Hard disk drives have a life-span which averages around five years, although it will vary from make to make. Eventually, any hard disk drive will fail and when it does, anything stored on it is likely to be lost. Obviously, this is a very serious problem.

To safeguard yourself against this problem, you should take regular backups from your hard disk. A backup is a copy of files from your hard disk to another storage medium like floppy disks, tape streamer, Iomega Zip disks or Jaz cartridge.

When you run Microsoft Backup, the Backup Wizard launches. This helps you create your first backup job. 'Job' is the name Backup gives to an association of backup settings, e.g:

- which files should be backed up

- where the resulting backup file should be stored

- whether the backup file should be compressed (a technique which results in much more data being stored in a given space)

Working with jobs makes carrying out backup and restore operations even easier.

When the Backup Wizard runs for the first time, it first checks whether you have any 'backup devices' (e.g. tape streamers) installed.

| Click on Backup from Start button, Programs, Accessories, System Tools. Or run it from Disk Properties.

If you've already created jobs and want to open one of them now, click Open an existing backup job instead of following steps 2-8.

In the Open Backup Job dialog, double-click the job you want to backup. In the Microsoft Backup window, make any necessary alterations, then click on Start. Finally, follow step 11.

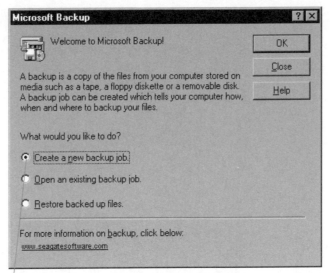

2 Click on Create a new backup job. Then click on OK.

Click here instead, to back up files on all your drives.

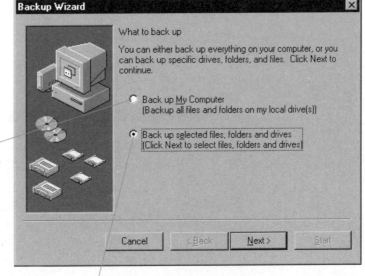

3 Click on Back up selected files, folders and drives. Then click on Next.

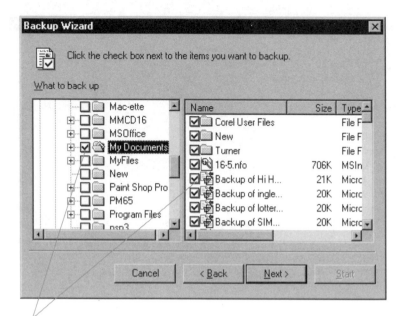

4 Select files or folders to backup. Click on the little box in front of a file/ folder to select it for backup, so that a blue tick ☑ appears inside. If only some files are selected from a folder the tick is greyed out ☑. To deselect, click again. Finally, click on Next.

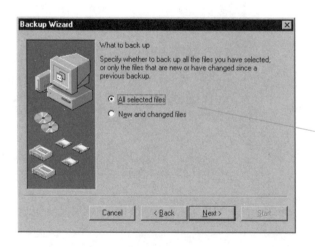

5 Select one of these, then click on Next.

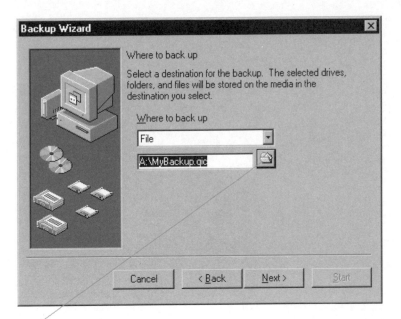

6 Click here.

7 Click on the arrow – select the destination drive/folder combination. Then click on <u>O</u>pen.

If you want, change the default filename here:

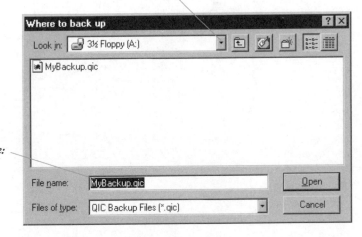

8 Select this to have the integrity of the backup file verified.

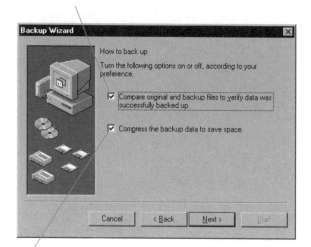

9 Select this to have the backup file compressed. Then click Next.

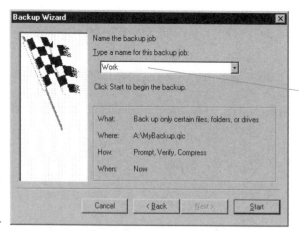

If your backup does not fit onto one floppy disk, feed in new floppies when prompted and number them sequentially.

10 Name the backup job, then click on Start.

11 When the backup is complete, click on OK in the message which launches, then OK in the Backup Progress dialog. Press Alt+F4 to close Backup.

Index

h

Hard disk
   Compressing   168–169
   Defragmenting   166–167
   Turning off   178
Help   15–17
   On-line technical support   20–21
   Product assistance
      Via Windows Update   173
   Shortcuts   16–17
   Topic window   15
   Troubleshooters   18–19, 124, 169

i

IMAP   97
Inbox. *See* Outlook Express
Installing
   Programs   50
   Windows components   51, 116
Internet
   Browsing   107–112
      With the Address Bar   64
   Channels. *See* Channels
   Connection Wizard
      Running   104–105
   Explorer. *See* Internet Explorer
   Logging on to   64, 105–106
   Overview   9, 104
   People
      Finding   105
   Searching   108, 116
   Web pages
      Creating   113–114
      Formatting   115
      Printing   112
      Publishing   116
      Saving   115
      Subscribing to   111
   Internet Explorer   9, 107, 109
      Toolbar   63
   Internet Settings   104

k

Keyboard
   Changing settings for   145
Kodak Imaging   153, 157

l

Links Toolbar
   Switching to Address Bar   65
   Switching to Standard Buttons toolbar   65
Logging off. *See* Windows 98, Multiple users, Logging off
Lost file fragments   164

m

Magnifier. *See* Accessibility Features, Microsoft Magnifier
Mail messages. *See* Outlook Express, Mail
Maintenance Wizard   8, 22, 163
   Running   170–171
Media Player
   Playing ActiveMovie clips in   156
   Playing Audio CDs in   146, 156
   Playing clips in   156
   Starting   156
Menus   26
Monitors
   Turning off   178
   Using more than one   8, 138
Mouse
   Changing settings for   144
   Using   9
MS-DOS applications (running)   54
Multimedia   146
   Live video/audio material
      Accessing on the Internet   147
   Playing Audio/Movie clips. *See* Media Player